Delicious Dishes for Diabetics

About the Author

Robin Ellis is best known as having starred in the BBC classic serial, *Poldark*, playing Captain Ross Poldark. It is widely regarded as one of the most popular British costume dramas ever produced. Other TV and film appearances have included roles in *Fawlty Towers*, *Elizabeth R*, *Blue Remembered Hills*, *The Europeans* and *Heartbeat*.

In 1999 Robin was diagnosed with Type 2 diabetes. Although he had no symptoms, he took the diagnosis seriously as his mother suffered with Type 1 diabetes for 35 years. In the same year he and his wife, Meredith, moved to southwest France where he has become known locally as the "*Anglais*" who cooks! By changing the way he ate and taking more exercise, Robin was able to control his blood sugar sufficiently to avoid taking medication for six years.

In this wonderful recipe collection Robin shares his favourite dishes so that other Type 2 diabetics and their families can enjoy the benefits of a healthy Mediterranean style of cooking.

There's an old Basque saying:
"To know how to eat is to know enough."

Delicious Dishes for Diabetics

Eating Well with Type-2 Diabetes

Robin Ellis

Skyhorse Publishing

Skyhorse Publishing books may be purchased in bulk at special discounts for sales promotion, corporate gifts, fund-raising, or educational purposes. Special editions can also be created to specifications. For details, contact the Special Sales Department, Skyhorse Publishing, 307 West 36th Street, 11th Floor, New York, NY 10018 or info@skyhorsepublishing.com.

Skyhorse® and Skyhorse Publishing® are registered trademarks of Skyhorse Publishing, Inc.®, a Delaware corporation.

www.skyhorsepublishing.com

10 9 8 7 6 5 4 3 2 1

Library of Congress Cataloging-in-Publication Data is available on file.
ISBN 978-1-61608-458-5 (pbk. : alk. paper)

Ellis, Robin, 1942-
Delicious Dishes for Diabetics : Eating Well with Type-2 Diabetes / Robin Ellis.
p. cm.
Includes index.

Printed in China

Praise from Those Who Have Enjoyed Robin's Dishes

Carmen Callil, publisher and author:
"Robin Ellis learned to cook at his mother's knee. This unique book is rich with a lifetime's experience of wonderful cooking in the Mediterranean way. His recipes open up a world of delicious, healthy eating which everyone will love. An instant classic."

Brian Cox, Scottish actor:
"Of course I am biased! Robin is a very old and dear friend! Even so, he is simply one of the best cooks ever. Why? His cuisine is always a delicious culinary paradox, Strong and delicate with an exquisite balance of flavours. One of the truly great treats of my life is a meal prepared by Robin – with the commitment, love and detail of a great actor preparing for a classical role. Once tasted, never forgotten!"

Lindsay Duncan, actress:
"Robin is the perfect cook to have as a friend. He loves food, cooks superbly and likes nothing more than sharing his food with as many people as he can get round a table. Generosity is at the heart of good cooking and Robin cooks to give pleasure. It always works."

Louise Fletcher, Academy-Award-winning actress (*One Flew Over the Cuckoo's Nest*):
"To have Sunday lunch at Robin's and to go home with his recipes is the perfect southwest France Sunday. Oh, let there be many more Sundays in the kitchen with Robin.

"Robin's cooking and Robin's recipes: simple, fresh and simply glorious."

Romaine Hart, cinema-owner (Screen on the Green/the Hill/Baker Street):
"Robin's cooking did what five different medications failed to do: bring down my high blood pressure. I suffered a stroke and no medication brought my blood pressure below 177/70. After staying only one week with Robin and eating his delicious meals, it came down to 120/59. Now home, my challenge is to reproduce his way of eating. With the help of this cook book, I am sure I can."

Sir Derek Jacobi, actor (Emmy, BAFTA, Olivier and Tony Awards):
"While not suffering from diabetes myself, I can highly recommend Robin's delicious recipes, some of which I have had the pleasure of sampling at his table in France. The recipes have all the richness of classical Mediterranean cooking. Enjoy yourselves as I have with this mouth-watering cornucopia!"

Michael Pennington, actor and author:
"Robin Ellis has the gift of writing recipes that you can taste as you read them. As if his acting weren't enough, he's now given us a marvellous book – without any pretension or carry-on, just deep affection and knowledge. Absolutely delicious."

Eva Marie Saint, Hollywood legend, Academy-Award and Emmy winner:
"Robin Ellis is a superb chef! His cookbook is filled with delicious and healthy recipes even for people like me who are not diabetics."

Tim Pigott-Smith, actor:
"It is always a joy to visit Le Presbytère. It is the most beautiful house, which reflects the calm of its isolated position and the nearby chapel. At the centre of this old building – whose thick walls guarantee that you can find relative cool even on the hottest day – is the small crowded kitchen.

"The sight of Robin – fully apronned, glasses strung round his neck, peacefully looking for spices, strolling out into the courtyard for a fresh fig to enliven a salad, or hunched over a saucepan stirring a fortifying soup – is surprising for anyone who remembers him striding across the stage at Stratford, or riding round Cornwall. However, it is here where he has truly found himself, in this house and in this room. As my wife Pam and I have been privileged to do many times, you can now enjoy its proceeds."

Imelda Staunton, actress:
"How can food this good be this good for you!"

Timberlake Wertenbaker, playwright (*Our Country's Good*):
"I've used Robin's recipes again and again. They're elegant, delicious, imaginative and easy to use.

"The Basques are great cooks and giving a dinner in the Basque Country is scary. One also eats very late so no one wants anything too heavy. I always use one of Robin's recipes and end up with nothing but compliments and a demand for the recipe.

" 'An English woman who can cook tuna!' someone said to me in complete astonishment. Of course, the recipe was Robin's."

Contents

Appreciations

I realize how lucky I am to have a cookbook published in these cash-strapped days, and I want to acknowledge the help and encouragement given by people in making this book possible.

First to thank is my editor Judith Mitchell, who has been a positive force and a patient guide, and it has been a pleasure to piece it together with her.

I am so grateful to Francia White, our friend in New York, who enthusiastically sent an outline of the book to her friend Paula Breslich in London, whom I also thank for forwarding it to Constable & Robinson. It would not have happened without them.

Hope James has designed three kitchens for me over the years, so it is appropriate that her lovely sketches adorn the book and let it breathe.

I also want to thank Paige Weaver for her cover photo, which invites people to open the book and try the recipes.

Meredith Wheeler, my dear wife and "taster in chief", has been my constant lunch and dinner companion.

When I thought to call a previous attempt, "Cooking for Meredith" it was entirely fitting; that is what I have been doing for twenty-five years and it has been a labour of love. I'm writing this on St Valentine's day by the way!

Thank you, Meredith, for your candour and enthusiasm; and for all the hard work and enterprise you've shown in driving this thing forward.

My thanks too to Holly Brady in California – who threw herself into promoting the book in the US with such wonderful élan.

Many others, knowingly or not, have had a hand in the birth of this book, and must be mentioned:

Brother Jack and sister-in-law Christine Kavanagh have steadily filled the kitchen shelves with the latest cookbooks at Christmas and birthdays. My nephew Theo's appetite for quail has spurred me on!

Theresa Hallgarten has been wonderfully generous with her time and expert advice; she also inspired the construction of the larder off the kitchen, which now begs the question – what on earth did I do with everything before!

Donald Douglas' imaginative soups are beautiful and tasty. Charlotte Fraser, whose cooking has been an inspiration, and her husband Nick have been generous hosts and dining partners.

So too Janet and John Willis, Lindsay Duncan and Hilton McRae, and Tari Mandair and Marc Urquhart. To these and many others, *merci* and *à bientôt*!

Introduction

This book is written for people who love food, enjoy cooking and wish to continue those pleasures despite a diagnosis of Type 2 diabetes.

It is also for those people who love them – because the Mediterranean way of eating is healthy for everyone.

In terms of food, though I live in France, my heart is in Italy. (It has all to do with fresh ingredients prepared *simply*.) One of my favourite places to eat in Florence is *Mario's* – a small family-run café near the wonderful St. Lorenzo food market. A modest place – only open for lunch – but always packed with marketers and those in the know. Often complete strangers are wedged together at the same tiny table. Last visit, I ordered their grilled veal chop with herbs and a plate of white beans with olive oil. Simple – yet sublime!

That is how I like to eat and to cook. This book is an anthology of recipes I have collected over the years that I have found reliable – not fussy or difficult. The dishes have a Mediterranean flavour – favouring olive oil, garlic and tomatoes as basic ingredients.

This is not a diet cookbook; rather it's a "way of eating and cooking" cookbook. There is something temporary implied about following a diet – like "taking the medicine"; it'll be over soon and one can get back to normal life. The way of eating in this book *is* normal life!

Though I had no symptoms, a routine blood test in 1999 turned up an elevated level of glucose. Shortly after being diagnosed with Type 2 diabetes, a friend recommended Michel Montignac's book, *Dine Out and Lose Weight,* now re-titled *Eat Yourself Slim and Stay Slim!* I found it very helpful. He too emphasized the importance of changing one's "way of eating" rather than dieting.

Montignac was from south-western France – coincidentally where I too live – which has a culture where eating well is central to a good life. One of the attractions of his eating plan is that it allows drinking wine (in moderation) as well as eating a couple of small squares of high cacao dark chocolate. Oh happy day!

As a young man, Montignac struggled with his weight. After working as a manager in the pharmaceutical industry, he left to develop his theory of why people put on weight and how to prevent it.

He was a pioneer in using the glycemic index of foods, which measures the effect of carbohydrates on blood sugar levels (how quickly carbohydrates turn to glucose in the blood) to help people

lose weight. Controlling one's weight is a primary concern for people with diabetes.

Montignac believed that increases in weight are caused by the high sugar content in some carbohydrate foods which encourages the body to store unwanted fat, rather than a high calorie intake.

My mother died of a heart attack, linked to her long struggle with Type 1 diabetes, aged 67, so I took my condition seriously from the start. Inspired by Michel Montignac's books and those of others, I adjusted my way of eating.

Out went white bread, white pasta and rice. Some root vegetables like potatoes, parsnips and beets also had to be avoided.

Rather than feeling deprived, this opened up new culinary paths – the discovery of the *sweet potato*, for instance. There are no excluded foods that I miss, though I don't have a sweet tooth, and I confess to looking for wholewheat pizzas on menus occasionally!

This adjustment, combined with regular walks and gentle yoga, reduced my blood sugar levels significantly. For years I avoided taking medicine for diabetes, simply by improving my diet and increasing my level of exercise.

Though Type 2 diabetes is not curable, it can be controlled without too much sacrifice.

Of course, it helped that I liked to cook and in fact had been a keen cook for years. That too goes back to my mother.

I grew up in the 1940s and 1950s in post-war austerity Britain. Food rationing only came to an end in 1954, when I was 12 years old. (In America rationing ended eight years earlier in 1946!)

My father worked for British Railways and had a modest income, with a wife and three young boys to support, so Ma had to be a good manager of the food budget. I remember queuing with her at the Sainsbury's grocery store in Golders Green in north London for what seemed like hours. We would wait at one counter to buy half a pound of butter, then queue on the other side of the aisle for a pound of tomatoes and stand in yet another line for bacon. Perhaps waiting resentfully in all those lines unconsciously instilled in me an appreciation of *quality* and the importance of spending time searching it out.

I do the same thing now, visiting our local French open-air market at least three times a week, standing in queues at the cheese stall, the fishmonger, the organic vegetable grower. Buying local produce from the vendors I have come to know over 20 years is one of the great pleasures of life in rural France, where our nearest town, Castres, has four open-air market days a week, plus another evening market for organic produce.

As well as a good manager, my mother, Molly, was a good cook. She collected recipes from newspapers and magazines and pasted them into a large, blue foolscap notebook. She would also write out recipes and pass them on. I have her recipe for *Smoked Mackerel Pâté*, written in her clear flowing hand, pasted into my large, *red* foolscap notebook. I collect recipes now and enjoy passing them on.

Molly loved to cook and to entertain. Thanks to her I grew up enjoying well-prepared simple food, eaten with family and friends around the kitchen table. She made her own marmalade with Seville oranges in February and started the traditional English Christmas pudding in September. We had individual Yorkshire puddings with roast beef on special Sundays with bread soaked in the "goodness" – the natural juices from the joint.

Often on a Sunday night, I'd give her a break and cook my "Special" – *Macaroni Cheese* with sliced tomato, grilled on top.

I'd bring everything into the living room on a tray table. Brother Peter was just six in 1954 and would be in bed; brother Jack (also now an actor) wasn't on the scene until June the following year, so Ma, Pa and I would sit in front of the fire and listen to Mary Martin in *South Pacific* singing *I'm Gonna Wash That Man Right Out of My Hair* on 78s on Pa's top-of-the-range gramophone.

Those convivial meals with my parents were the start of my love affair with food – and eating with others, in an agreeable social setting. In that same year, 1954, when rationing ended in Britain, Dad took advantage of concessionary rail travel for British Rail employees in Europe and took us all to the Costa Brava on Spain's Mediterranean coast for a two-week holiday.

It was a bold destination for that era, long before British package tours hit the scene. I ate garlic for the first time, eggs cooked in olive

oil, sun-ripened peaches and tomatoes unlike any we ever bought at Sainsbury's. This exposure to a completely different cuisine made a deep impression on me – and, of course, my mother. We spent two weeks in Lloret del Mar, rather bizarrely sharing the beach and sun with Franco's military police who wore strange helmets and carried menacing machine guns; very different from the beaches at Woolacombe Sands or in Cornwall. As an impressionable 12-year-old English schoolboy, I concluded that there was an interesting world elsewhere...

That year, 1954, also saw the publication of Elizabeth David's seminal cookbook, *Italian Food* – a follow up to her first book, *Mediterranean Cooking*. Her books were to underwrite a cooking revolution in Britain and have inspired me for years.

The Reluctant Cookbook Writer

Friends and family have been urging me to "write a cookbook" for as long as I can remember. I never felt comfortable with the idea. I would feel a fraud claiming that such-and-such a recipe is *mine*, because I added an extra two tablespoons of thyme to the recipe, instead of parsley, for example!

Many people (especially my wife!) thought this was just an excuse not to attempt a book. Then one day two summers ago, the English playwright and friend, Timberlake Wertenbaker emailed from her holiday home in the Basque country, asking for recipe ideas. She had people coming to dinner and was temporarily stumped. I had written out certain oft-requested recipes by this time and stored them on the computer, so it was no trouble to email them. I started to write up recipes as I cooked them, and discovered that I enjoyed the experience. Lo and behold, soon I had more than one hundred.

So when the opportunity came up to collect them altogether in this book to be aimed at fellow "Type Two-ers" I felt ready and eager to accept.

Most are from books, magazines and newspapers (collected just as my mother did). A few recipes come from friends (some of whom have written their own cookbooks!).

Collecting them is a passion. I make no claims to being an inventive chef, creating new dishes. I'm an actor after all. I've always been more comfortable working from scripts than improvising. I'm an interpreter rather than a creator. But I do have a compulsive urge to search out *workable* dishes that also fit into my "way of eating" needs.

They have also had to pass the ultimate test – *Meredith [my wife] Approved!*

Sometimes thumbing through a cookbook that I haven't consulted for a while, I come across a comment written in big round easily-recognizable letters along the margin of a recipe: *Very good!* or *Mind-boggling!* or simply *YES!!!* I feel it's fairly safe to try these again.

Incidentally, the *mind-boggling* recipe is for a crushed garlic and walnut sauce to be served with grilled duck breast (page 65).

So with a nod to all the cooks whose recipes have inspired me for the past 40 years, I offer this collection for family, friends, and fellow "Type-Two-ers": over one hundred recipes that I like – and if I can cook them so can you.

With special thanks to some of the professional cooks who have inspired me, starting with Elizabeth David, the wonderful Marcella Hazan, Mireille Johnston, Jenny Baker, Anna del Conte, Valentina Harris, Rose Elliot, Claudia Roden and more recently, Rose Gray and Ruth Rogers, Jamie Oliver and Nigel Slater.

Robin Ellis
Lautrec, France
August 2011

Ingredients and the Mediterranean Way of Eating

Always use the best you can afford and find. Eating *in* is cheaper than eating *out* – so you can legitimately cut yourself some slack and spend a bit extra.

Research now shows that the Mediterranean way of eating is one of the healthiest on the planet.

Key elements include:

- Eating plenty of fresh fruit and vegetables
- Eating whole grains, brown rice, wholewheat pasta and legumes
- Seasoning food with herbs and spices (so less salt is required)
- Including nuts and seeds (dry roasting brings out the flavour)
- Reducing the amount of red meat in the diet
- Eating fish or shellfish at least twice a week
- Limiting dairy products (use low-fat versions)
- Cooking with olive oil rather than butter

Ever since eating those eggs in Spanish olive oil on the Costa Brava, I have always favoured olive oil over butter for cooking and, as you will see, I cook almost exclusively with it now. This always means cold processed Extra Virgin olive oil.

Nowadays I rarely like the flavour of butter in cooked food – though sometimes a mixture of oil and butter is useful. Rounding off a sauce by folding in a little diced cold butter to give it a sheen – for example, to the quail in balsamic vinegar dish (page 132) – adds a touch of glamour to which I'm not averse. However generally speaking, olive oil is king.

Stock is a touchy subject in some households. It's simple for me: I have never got into the habit of making fresh stock. I've been using organic vegetable stock cubes (available in most health food stores) for years. I no longer use chicken stock cubes. Their flavour is too marked for me now. For those who have the time and energy to make homemade stock, I tip my hat in admiration. Store bought cubes and powder are what I use in these recipes.

It's important to *taste* food as it cooks, to judge the seasoning and the doneness. *Sample* the simmering tomato sauce to see if it's concentrated enough. *Test* the green bean to see how much longer it must cook. *Bite on* the strand of spaghetti, to make sure it's done to your liking.

Be careful when handling fresh chillies as they can sting. Wash your hands thoroughly after handling them.

A pair tongs is essential and a small wooden tasting spoon is nice too.

American readers should follow the cup measurements when measuring volumes of liquid since UK (not US) pints are used in the recipes.

Bon appétit – Buon appetito!

1

Soups

Recently we've enjoyed having soup for supper. As the name suggests, this is the traditional way of eating an evening meal. Eating lightly at the end of the day is obviously better for the digestion and makes it easier for the body to settle into the sleep mode.

Soups make a lovely lunch too – followed by a salad.

Many soups are quick and simple to make. They keep and the taste improves in the fridge, so they can be wheeled out for company. Summer soups served chilled, like Donald's Cold Cucumber Soup (page 14), make life easier when entertaining.

Bean Soup with Tomato, Garlic and Pasta

Serves 4

This satisfying soup is based on one in Elizabeth Romer's lovely book, *The Tuscan Year: Life and Food in an Italian Family*. Her account of the Cerroti family's daily existence is a very good read and full of authentic seasonal recipes.

4 tbsp olive oil
2 onions – chopped small
2 sticks of celery – chopped small
3 cloves of garlic – finely chopped
100 g/4 oz smoked bacon/pancetta – use unsmoked if you prefer – chopped small
4 tbsp flat leaf parsley – chopped
1 x 450 g/16 oz can tomatoes – drained and chopped
350 g/12 oz tinned/jarred white beans – drained, rinsed and puréed
570 ml/1 pint/2½ cups vegetable stock – more if you like
150 g/6 oz short wholewheat pasta – penne, farfalle
salt and pepper

1. Heat the olive oil in a large saucepan. Add the onions, celery, garlic, bacon and parsley, and turn them in the oil. Cook them over a gentle heat until the vegetables are tender and the bacon is colouring up – this is the "taste engine" of the soup and needs some time – at least 20 minutes.
2. Add the tomatoes and mix them in and allow to meld for a good 10 minutes.

3. Add the beans and mix in. Again, cook gently for 10 minutes. These stages are important for a good depth of flavour and shouldn't be rushed.

4. The soup should look beautiful now – with a warm glow. Add half the stock and let it meld in.

5. Add the pasta and the rest of the stock and cook the pasta in the soup. It may take a little longer than pasta normally does; I put a lid on at this point to help. Be careful that this thick and unctuous soup does not stick and burn. If you prefer it looser, add more stock and cook on a little to incorporate it.

6. Check the seasoning, adding salt and pepper to taste – but remembering that the bacon and stock can be salty.

7. Serve with grated Parmesan cheese and swirls of olive oil.

Donald's Cold Cucumber Soup

Serves 2 ladles each for 5 people; you may wish you'd made more because this soup is something!

Donald Douglas, who, as Captain McNeil, chased me in vain, through many *Poldark* episodes, has finally come to terms with the hopelessness of his pursuit and, in fact, lives close by. He's much better at making soup than he ever was as a soldier and, as a way of letting bygones be bygones, has given me permission to include this wonderful summer soup!

2 tbsp olive oil
1 flat tsp salt – be careful, the stock may be salty
2 crushed cloves of garlic
zest of a small lemon
juice of ½ lemon
1 large cucumber
500 g/16 oz yogurt – I use fat-free, Donald uses Greek which is richer
1 organic vegetable stock cube
chopped parsley

1. In a large bowl mix the first five ingredients.
2. Peel the cucumber, leaving some strips of green. Grate it into the bowl. Add the yogurt.
3. Make 350 ml/12 fl oz/1½ cups white stock with the stock cube.
4. When cool, add to the bowl. Add some chopped parsley and mix all the ingredients thoroughly.
5. Chill in the fridge, preferably overnight. It's a good idea to put the soup bowls in the fridge for a couple of hours before serving.
6. Stir the soup thoroughly and place an ice cube in each bowl. I like to add 2 peeled prawns and a pinch of parsley too.

Fennel Soup

Serves 4

This is adapted from Valentina Harris's *Italian Farmhouse* book and is wonderfully simple. The ingredients speak for its authenticity. Serve it over wholewheat or rye toast, stroked with a bruised clove of garlic.

4 large bulbs of fennel – bruised bits removed, halved top to
    toe, then cut side down, each half finely sliced
3 cloves of garlic – finely chopped
2 tbsp flat-leaved parsley – chopped
2 good tbsp olive oil
salt and pepper
1.2 litres/2 pints/5 cups vegetable stock

1. Combine the fennel, garlic, parsley and oil in a large pan with a pinch of salt, and turn over in the oil.
2. Cook gently, turning to avoid burning, for about 7–8 minutes.
3. Add the stock and bring to the boil.
4. Simmer gently until the fennel is completely tender. Check for salt, and season generously with black pepper.

Minestrone

Serves 6

Of course, minestrone is Italian for soup! Here's a version we often enjoy in the winter months, made with or without smoked bacon.

1 tbsp olive oil
100 g/4 oz smoked bacon – diced
1 large onion – peeled and chopped
2 large leeks – outer leaves removed, washed and sliced
2 celery stalks – bruised bits cut away, chopped
180 g/6 oz tinned or bottled white beans
255 g/9 oz tinned tomatoes
1 sweet potato – diced
1 large fennel bulb – outer layers removed, chopped in large dice
some cabbage (Savoy if possible) leaves, torn up
850 ml/1½ pints/3½ cups or more vegetable stock
small handful parsley, tied
salt and pepper

1. Heat the oil and add the bacon (if using). Let it brown gently.
2. Add the chopped onion, leeks, and celery (start with these in the oil if not using the bacon), mix them in well and let them sweat down for about 20 minutes. This slow sweating is what gives depth to the soup.
3. Add the beans to the sweated vegetables and mix them in. Do the same with the tomatoes, breaking them up a little.
4. Add the diced sweet potato and fennel.
5. Add the cabbage, the stock and the tied parsley. Season and bring gently to simmer, cover and cook at this gentle simmer for a good hour. The soup should be thick with vegetables. Add more stock if you need it.
6. Serve with a jug of the best olive oil you can muster.

Leek and Chickpea Soup

Serves 4

This is simple and delicious.

1 kg/2¼ lb leeks
3 tbsp olive oil
salt and pepper
450 g/1 lb (large jar or tin) chickpeas
850 ml/1½ pints/3½ cups vegetable or chicken stock
75 g/3 oz Parmesan cheese – freshly grated

1. Prepare the leeks by cutting away the damaged brown tops, leaving as much of the green as possible and trimming the root ends. To wash them effectively, cut them down centrally from the top to just above the root and wash thoroughly to clear any muddy residue. Slice them finely.
2. Heat the oil in a large saucepan and add the sliced leeks and some salt. How much salt depends on the saltiness of the stock to come, so be careful. Cover the pan and sweat the leeks over a low heat until they are nicely melted.
3. Add the drained and rinsed chickpeas and mix with the leeks.
4. Add the stock and cook uncovered for 15 minutes.
5. Take a couple of ladles from the pan, mush them and return to the pan. Add the Parmesan and freshly ground black pepper and mix in well.
6. Reheat and serve with more Parmesan on the side.

White Bean and Parsley Soup

Serves 4

My version of this serious bean soup from Marcella Hazan.

1 clove of garlic – peeled and chopped
8 tbsp olive oil
2 tbsp parsley – chopped
1 kg/36 oz canned or, preferably, bottled white beans – drained
  and rinsed
salt and pepper
250 ml/½ pint/1 cup vegetable stock
toasted wholewheat bread with a little olive oil

1. Sauté the garlic in the oil gently until it colours.
2. Add the parsley and stir a couple of times. Mix in the beans, salt and pepper.
3. Cover and cook gently for about 5 minutes to warm through.
4. Purée a quarter of the beans in a mixer and return with the stock to the pan. Simmer for another 5 minutes.
5. Check the seasoning. Serve over the toast with a swirl of olive oil in each bowl.

Swiss Chard, White Bean and Pasta Soup

Serves 4

This superb soup, based on a recipe by Marcella Hazan, is a meal in itself. It takes a little time but is well worth it.

450 g/1 lb Swiss chard – leaves separated from the stalks
1 tsp salt
850 ml/1½ pints/3½ cups water
6 tbsp olive oil
2 whole peeled cloves of garlic
2 anchovy fillets – mashed
sprig of fresh rosemary
350 g/12 oz cooked white tinned/bottled beans
black pepper
285 ml/½ pint/1¼ cups hot water with ½ stock cube dissolved in it
90 g/3 oz wholewheat pasta – penne, farfalle, fusilli, etc
30 g/1 oz grated Parmesan cheese

1. Soak and rinse the leaves and stalks of the chard – they must be clean. Cut the stalks into cork-length chunks and roughly chop the leaves.
2. Add the salt to the water and bring to the boil in a large saucepan. Put in the chard stalks first and cook them for a couple of minutes. Add the leaves and cook uncovered for another 3 minutes, until tender.
3. Remove the chard, keeping all the liquid for later use. It will serve as a good part of the soup liquid. Roughly chop the chard.

4. Heat the oil in a large pan and add the garlic. When it has browned, take the pan off the heat and add the anchovies and rosemary. Stir to dissolve the anchovies for a couple of minutes. Remove the garlic and rosemary. Turn the heat back on low and add the chard leaves and stalks. Turn them in the oil and cook for a couple of minutes.
5. Add the beans, turn in the oil, and cook them for a couple of minutes.
6. Pepper well. Perhaps add salt but be careful as anchovies are salty.
7. Add the chard water and the extra water with dissolved stock cube. When the water comes to the boil, add the pasta and cook until it is tender, covered to preserve the volume.
8. Turn off the heat and add the cheese.

2

Light Lunches and Starters

Elizabeth David elegantly established her choice for the perfect light lunch with the title of her book, *An Omelette and a Glass of Wine*. Omelettes feature regularly here at lunchtime and a slice of freshly made courgette frittata would be a delicious starter.

In summer, with the arrival of the green bean, the choice is expanded. A scattering of beans for each person (100 g/4 oz, say) with some good olive oil drizzled over them while they are still warm, and a thin slice of interesting toast (wholewheat walnut perhaps) would be enough; but you could add some halved cherry tomatoes, crumbled feta, or mashed anchovies.

Aubergine Slices with a Walnut and Garlic Spread

Serves 4

This lovely seasonal starter has the added advantage that you are able to prepare it beforehand.

2 large aubergines
salt
2 tbsp olive oil
2–3 tbsp wine vinegar

Sauce:
3–4 cloves of garlic – crushed with a little salt
60 g/2 oz walnuts – shelled; if you do this yourself, take care
   that no pieces of shell get left with the nuts
handful chopped parsley

1. Wash and cut the aubergines lengthwise into 1.5 cm/½ inch slices. Salt them slightly and put them in a colander for an hour or so, to drain off some of their bitter juice.
2. Dry them thoroughly and brush generously with olive oil on both sides. Heat the oven at 240°C/475°F/Gas Mark 9.
3. Put the aubergines on well-oiled foil in a shallow oven tray. Cook them in the oven for about 20 minutes to brown them, turning after 10 minutes.
4. While the aubergines are in the oven, make the sauce. Mix the crushed garlic with a tablespoon of olive oil. Chop the walnuts in a processor or pound them in a pestle and mortar.

5. Combine these two ingredients with the parsley in a bowl and add another tablespoon of oil. Mix well and check for salt.

6. Take the aubergines out of the oven, put them on a serving plate, brush with the vinegar and spread the delicious sauce on top. Serve cold.

Asparagus

Serves 4

Asparagus arrives in the market in France in early April – an Easter treat. Five or six spears are enough as a starter.

about 20 asparagus spears

1. Trim the rough base of the spears, making them all about the same length.
2. Choose a saucepan or sauté pan that will take them all lying horizontally, and that is wide enough to take a steamer basket. Fill with water to the depth of the basket. Place the asparagus horizontally in the basket and cover the pan. It's handy to cook an extra spear that you can use to test for "doneness".
3. Cooking for 6–8 minutes should be sufficient, depending on their thickness. Pierce the spare spear with the tip of a knife to test – or, better still, use your teeth!
4. Lay the asparagus out neatly on individual plates and pour a portion of the sauce on page 53 at the side. This is finger food for me – rolling the spears in the sauce is very pleasing!

Baked Sweet Potato with Fillings

Serves 4

It seems a contradiction in terms – they are called *sweet* potatoes, after all – but this vegetable is fine for diabetics; it has a different fibre make-up from the ordinary potato and a lower GI rating. It's delicious too!

2 medium-size sweet potatoes – evenly shaped; of course, you could also cook one per person

1. Heat the oven at 190°C/375°F/Gas Mark 5.
2. Lightly trace a circle lengthwise round the middle of the potatoes – just breaking the skin. This is to stop them bursting in the heat.
3. Place them high in the oven and cook for about an hour or until tender when pierced through. Remove from the oven and halve them lengthwise.

Possible Fillings:
1. Simple seasoning: salt and pepper – and olive oil.
2. A yogurt of choice. I like low-fat. (See method for making it thicker, on page 181.) Depotting the yogurt and whisking it first makes it more agreeable to eat. You can add a little crushed garlic to it and/or some cumin powder or whatever you like, of course.
3. Gently sautéed diced bacon goes well – smoked or green.
4. The broccoli and anchovy recipe (page 30) is also good – it's your choice!

Cauliflower in Tomato Sauce with Chorizo Sausage

Serves 3 or 4

Try this on the chickpea pancake (socca), page 174 – for a light supper.

450 g/1 lb cauliflower florets – not too large
2 tbsp olive oil
1 onion – chopped
2 cloves of garlic – chopped
1 pulped anchovy fillet
12 oz/350 g tinned tomatoes – drained and chopped
a dash of red wine – optional
½ spicy chorizo sausage – diced
1 extra tbsp olive oil
salt and pepper

1. Cook the cauliflower florets in salted water at a simmer until just soft. Drain and then set them aside.
2. Heat the oil in a sauté pan and add the onion and garlic. Cook gently until they soften.
3. Add the anchovy and stir it in.
4. Add the tomatoes and stir them in.
5. Add the dash of wine. Cook until the sauce is thick and unctuous – about 20 minutes.

6. Meanwhile, in a small frying pan sauté the chorizo dice gently in the extra olive oil – releasing the fat and letting it turn colour a little.
7. Add the dice to the sauce and fold in the cauliflower.
8. Cook for a further 2 or 3 minutes for the flavours to meld.
9. Check the seasoning and add salt and pepper to taste.
10. Serve over quinoa or, as suggested above, on the socca pancake. A simple green salad would be a good addition.

Broccoli with Anchovy Sauce on Toast

Serves 4

This makes a tasty starter or a light supper.

500 g/1 lb broccoli – cut into smallish pieces
4 tbsp olive oil
2 cloves of garlic – peeled and finely sliced
2 small chillies – deseeded and chopped small
8 anchovy fillets – preferably from salted anchovies (they dissolve more easily)
pepper
4 slices of wholewheat bread
1 clove of garlic – halved
2 lemons cut in pieces

1. Steam the broccoli until just tender – it's going to be cooked further – and retain the water.
2. Heat the oil in a pan large enough to take the broccoli. Gently brown the garlic, add the chillies, then, off the heat, add and dissolve the anchovies.
3. Add some of the hot water from the broccoli cooking to make a sauce – about half a small wine glass. Fold the broccoli into this sauce and carefully mix. Continue to cook for a further 5 minutes.
4. Season well with pepper.
5. Toast the bread slices. Rub them with the garlic halves. Serve the broccoli on the toast. You could pop a sun-dried tomato or two on top.
6. Serve lemon pieces on the side for squeezing.

Eggs Poached in a Tomato Sauce

Serves 4

A very simple and surprising dish based on one in Valentina Harris's book of food from southern Italy – you are bound to have the ingredients in the cupboard.

450 g/1 lb tinned tomatoes – drained and chopped
1 tsp salt and pepper from the mill
3 tbsp olive oil
8 eggs

1. Put the tomatoes in a small saucepan, add the salt and some pepper, and a couple of tablespoons of water and bring them to the simmer.
2. Cover and cook for 30 minutes – stirring from time to time.
3. Heat the oven at 180°C/350°F/Gas Mark 4.
4. Pass the rough sauce through a sieve.
5. Put the olive oil in a heated earthenware dish and pour the sauce over it.
6. Trying not to break them, crack the eggs carefully into the sauce, and season with a few twists from the pepper mill.
7. Put the dish into the oven. The eggs should take 7–10 minutes.
8. Serve with pieces of toast with olive oil sprinkled over and perhaps a salad.

Omelette with Cheese and Herbs

Serves 1

Add whatever filling you want – this is just the basic method.

2 free-range eggs
salt and pepper
a pinch of fresh herbs – finely chopped – parsley, thyme,
    rosemary, sage, mint, tarragon, chives – any of these or a
    mixture
a little olive oil or use butter if you prefer
1 tbsp Parmesan cheese – freshly grated

1. Heat an omelette pan gently to very hot.
2. Whisk the eggs lightly in a bowl.
3. Add a little salt and pepper and a pinch of the herbs.
4. Add the oil or butter to the pan. Allow it to get hot. Fold in the egg mix and cook over a high heat. With a wooden spoon, tack round the circumference of the egg mix, releasing a little of the liquid each time to build a quilty-like texture to the cooking omelette.
5. Sprinkle on the cheese.
6. Remove from the heat when you have a creamy and scrummy-looking item that looks just cooked. Fold as you like and serve immediately with a little extra Parmesan sprinkled down the fold of the omelette.

Roast Asparagus

Serves 4

Asparagus is wonderful, but even in its short season it can get a bit repetitive! This is a handy alternative way; quick and easy with the thinner type. The addition of thyme comes from the River Café.

2 tbsp olive oil
500 g/1 lb thinnish asparagus
2 tbsp fresh thyme leaves
salt

1. Heat the oven at 220°C/425°F/Gas Mark 7.
2. Heat the oil in a shallow baking tray.
3. Turn the asparagus in it and sprinkle over the thyme and some salt. The roasting time depends on the thickness of the asparagus: about 5 or 6 minutes for thin and a bit longer for the fatter size. It should crisp up a bit.
4. Serve with extra oil and salt or you could try it with the simple sauce for fish on page 58.

Rice and Spinach Torte

Serves 4 as lunch or more as a starter

Based on Marcella Hazan's version of a classic, this is very useful as there is no pastry. You can cook the spinach, rice and onions well in advance, the night before even; then it turns into an assembly job and as such is therapeutic!

1 kg/2¼ lb spinach – washed carefully
200 g/7 oz basmati long-grain rice
1 medium onion – chopped
25 g/1 oz butter
4 tbsp olive oil
¼ tsp grated nutmeg
50 g/2 oz grated Parmesan cheese
salt and pepper
4 eggs
25 g/1 oz breadcrumbs – rye or 100 per cent wholewheat
a loose-bottomed torte (oven) tin – 25 cm/10 inches

1. Cook the spinach in the water clinging to it after washing, covered, over a gentle heat – until it has wilted completely – about 10 minutes.
2. When it's cool enough, squeeze as much water out of the ball as you can and roughly chop it.
3. Cook the rice in a saucepan, in 570 ml/1 pint/2½ cups of water, covered and over a low heat – it will take about 25 minutes. Test it for tenderness; drain and leave to cool.
4. Cook the onion in the butter and oil in a large sauté pan over a medium heat until it is a lively brown.

5. Add the cooled spinach and rice to the onion and cook on low heat for about 4 minutes, turning to mix and coat well with the oil and butter. Leave to cool.
6. Heat the oven at 230°C/450°F/Gas Mark 8.
7. Add the nutmeg and half the cheese to the mixture. Season this mix carefully with salt and pepper – tasting and turning as you go – the salt should just come through. Turn in the eggs singly.
8. Butter or oil the torte tin and sprinkle half the breadcrumbs in the base. Now turn the mix into it and smooth over the surface. Mix the remaining crumbs and cheese and sprinkle them over the surface. Dribble olive oil over this.
9. Bake in the top of the oven for 15 minutes.
10. Serve tepid, perhaps with a tomato sauce.

Sardines with a Fresh Mint, Anchovy and Chilli Dressing

Serves 4

A variation of Skye Gyngell's recipe, this works well as a light summer lunch served with a tomato salad. Two sardines, each served on a bed of sliced ripe tomatoes, would make a tasty starter.

16 very fresh sardines – butterfly filleted (see below) or ask your fishmonger
2 anchovy fillets
1 fresh red chilli – finely chopped
2–3 tbsp fresh mint – finely chopped
4 tbsp/80 ml/3 fl oz olive oil
sea salt and pepper

1. Heat the oven at 180°C/350°F/Gas Mark 4 if using.
2. Filleting is a bit of a business but rewarding. You'll need a chopping board and plenty of kitchen paper. Have a pair of scissors to hand and a plate to receive the fillets. Make sure there are no scales left on the fish, then with the head in your left hand and the body in your right, gently pull the head off and as much of the innards as possible from the tail end. Use the scissors to snip along the belly, then with your left thumb coax out the rest of the innards. Place the fish, belly down, on the board and press gently up and down the backbone with both thumbs. Flatten the fish as much as you can with three fingers of both hands. Lift and snip off the small fin, then snip the backbone at the tail end and, with the left hand, draw it carefully away from the body, taking care not to take too much of the flesh with it. Voila! You have a butterfly fillet.

36

3. To make the dressing, pound the anchovies in a pestle and mortar. Add the chilli and mint, and whisk in the olive oil; set aside.

4. Sprinkle the salt and a few twists of the pepper mill over the fillets, then either cook in the oven for 15 minutes or in a pan, which will need no oil as the sardines will give off enough as they cook. Heat the pan to hot before adding the seasoned sardines, ensuring you place them well apart, skin-side down. Cook without turning for 2–3 minutes. When done, the skin should be crisp and the flesh will have lost its translucence.

5. Spoon over the dressing and serve immediately on a warmed plate.

Roast Ratatouille

Serves 4

Adapted from Delia Smith's recipe, this is useful as a starter or light main course. It also looks good in summer served with the salmon fillet on page 112 with some green beans.

450 g/1 lb cherry tomatoes – vary the colour if you see them
2 courgettes – cut into 2.5 cm/1 inch dice
1 aubergine – cut roughly the same as the courgettes
2 yellow or red peppers – deseeded and cut as above
1 red onion – chopped as above
2 large cloves of garlic – finely chopped
3 tbsp olive oil
some basil leaves
salt and pepper

1. Heat the oven at its hottest, i.e. 240–250°C/475–500°F/Gas Mark 9.
2. Put all the vegetables in a large bowl, sprinkle over the garlic, mix in the oil and the basil. Season with salt and pepper. Turn it all over thoroughly.
3. Fold all this carefully onto a large shallow roasting tin that you have already brushed with oil or covered in oiled foil; the vegetables must have room to catch the heat otherwise they will stew.
4. Place the tin on the highest rack of the oven. Roast for 20 minutes – check after 10 minutes for burning and "doneness" ("charred" is good, "burned" not so good!); roasting time will vary depending on the thickness of the vegetables and your oven.
5. Serve tapenade sauce with this if you like – it goes particularly well; and you could try adding some cubes of feta cheese for the last 10 minutes – thus calling in at various spots on the Mediterranean!

Fennel, White Bean and Parmesan Salad

Serves 4

Originating from Melrose and Morgan of Primrose Hill, London, this combination is enlivened by the lemony dressing – it's moreish! Another good lunch number for company.

Dressing
1 tbsp lemon juice and zest of the lemon
3 tbsp olive oil
salt and pepper

Salad
2 large fennel bulbs – outer parts removed and very finely sliced
1 x 400 g/14 oz jar/tin good quality white beans – drained and rinsed
½ small red onion – very finely sliced
handful red radishes – optional – thinly sliced
50 g/2 oz Parmesan cheese – very thinly shaved
2 tbsp chopped parsley
salt and pepper

1. Whisk the dressing ingredients together and taste.
2. Assemble the salad ingredients in order. Season and pour the dressing over.
3. Turn it all over carefully and sprinkle more parsley on top.

3
Salads

Salad can mean pretty much anything these days – imagination is the mother of invention!

The other day I ordered the mushroom salad from an Italian menu – on the recommendation of a friend. It was a simple idea, involving small field mushrooms finely sliced, shavings of Parmesan, some fresh thyme and a dressing of olive oil and lemon juice, with rocket leaves worked in, seasoned with salt and pepper. That was lunch and very good it was.

There are classic salads too, of course, and many ways of assembling them; here are some useful ones.

Chicory, Orange and Feta Salad

Serves 4 for lunch, 6 as a starter

It takes a little time to assemble this wonderful, fresh-tasting salad, adapted from the Moro stable – but it's worth the effort.

3 chicory bulbs – bruised outer leaves removed, the remaining leaves separated
2 juicy oranges – peel and pith carefully removed
½ small red onion – very thinly sliced
good handful of parsley – chopped
50 g/2 oz pitted Greek black olives – the juiciest you can find
100 g/4 oz shelled walnuts – dry roasted in a small pan
100 g/4 oz feta cheese
1 tbsp red wine vinegar
salt and pepper
4 tbsp olive oil
zest of a lemon

1. Choose the bowl you are going to serve the salad from. Place some chicory leaves round the circumference of the bowl.
2. Slice the oranges latitudinally – not too thinly – and lay the slices in the base of the bowl.
3. Scatter the rest of the chicory over the oranges.
4. Toss over the red onion.
5. Sprinkle on the parsley, the olives, the walnuts and the crumbled feta.
6. Whisk salt and pepper in the vinegar, then the oil.
7. Pour the dressing over the salad and scatter on the zest. After showing it off, turn it over in the dressing.

Fennel Salad with Parmesan Shavings

Serves 4

I'm serving this today with the salmon fishcakes (page 108) – it should cut their richness nicely.

4 fennel bulbs – tough outer layers removed, but keeping the soft green tufts
4 tbsp olive oil
1 lemon – juiced and zest
Parmesan cheese shavings
salt and pepper

1. Halve the fennel bulbs and lay the cut side down flat. Slice these halves finely and put them in a bowl.
2. Whisk the oil and lemon and pour over the fennel bulbs.
3. Add the Parmesan shavings.
4. Season generously but with care.
5. Turn the salad over several times to coat everything in the mix.
6. Turn into a serving bowl.
7. Sprinkle the chopped tufts of the fennel, some extra shavings of Parmesan, and the lemon zest on top and set aside to marinade for perhaps an hour if there's time.

A Roast Red Pepper Salad with "Edge"

Serves 4

Here's a nice gooey slightly piquant salad that profits from the addition of some flaked very fresh feta or goat's cheese. You could also add a few slices of thin pancetta for the last 10 minutes of cooking.

4 red peppers – cut in half lengthwise, deseeded and cut into strips
1 red chilli – not too hot, deseeded and cut into strips
4 tbsp extra-virgin olive oil
1 large or 2 medium red onions – peeled, cut in half and thickly sliced
2 cloves of garlic – peeled and sliced
2 tbsp balsamic vinegar
fresh basil

1. Heat the oven at 220°C/425°F/Gas Mark 7.
2. Line a shallow medium-sized oven tray with foil and brush with oil.
3. Fill it with the peppers and the chilli in a single layer. Dribble over 3 tablespoons of oil.
4. Leave in the oven for 20 minutes before spreading over the onion and garlic and cooking for a further 20 minutes. Everything should be charred in a nice way, i.e. edible!
5. Sprinkle over the balsamic and the torn basil and extra olive oil if you like.

Rocket, Celery, Garlic and Sautéed Chickpea Salad

Serves 4

This dish goes well with chicken breasts or served as a starter or salad in its own right.

1 celery heart – outer damaged sticks removed and the
   remaining stems sliced thin
100 ml/4 fl oz/6 tbsp extra-virgin olive oil
2 cloves of garlic – lightly crushed
1 x 400 g/14 oz tin of chickpeas – rinsed, with the thin skins
   slipped off if you have time
1 tbsp lemon juice
sea salt and black pepper
50 g/2 oz rocket leaves – coarsely chopped

1. Put the celery in the serving bowl of your choice.
2. Heat half the oil in a medium sauté pan and fry the garlic until
    it colours. Then remove it, and add the chickpeas, turning
    them in the oil and frying gently until they crisp a little.
3. Allow the chickpeas to cool, then add them to the celery.
4. Whisk the remaining oil and the lemon juice together, adding
    salt and a good amount of black pepper. Pour it over the
    salad, fold in the rocket leaves and turn over thoroughly.
5. Allow to stand for an hour before serving.

Salade Niçoise

Serves 4

Wonderfully useful salad for company on sunny days in summer. Everyone has their version of this classic. For me, the essentials are anchovies, eggs, olives, beans, tuna, ripe tomatoes, and a fair amount of garlic in the dressing, as shown on the front cover.

some crisp salad leaves
4 ripe tomatoes – peeled if you prefer
(pour boiling water over them and leave for 30 seconds) and
   quartered
½ large cucumber – peeled, quartered lengthwise and deseeded
1 large or several small spring onions – finely sliced
250 g/8 oz green beans – cooked to just tender
2–3 tins tuna – drained weight about 200–300 g/8–9 oz
handful Niçoise olives or black if not
4 freshly hard boiled eggs – halved
8 anchovy fillets
10 tbsp olive oil
2 cloves of garlic – mashed
salt and pepper
some basil, parsley and mint leaves – what's available really

1. Choose a serving dish large enough for a pretty display. Make a base of the salad leaves, followed by the tomatoes, cucumber and onion, and build from there. The eggs should be added last with a slice of anchovy on each.
2. Whisk the olive oil and garlic, add the salt and pepper and the herbs, and pour over.
3. Show off your handiwork. Then carefully turn over the salad in the dressing and serve – with a chilled rosé perhaps.

Salad of Escarole Lettuce with Spicy Chorizo

Serves 4

Based on a wonderful Moro Cookbook recipe.

leaves from an escarole lettuce – washed and spun dry
1 tbsp olive oil
1 spicy chorizo sausage – cut in half lengthwise and sliced into dice
100 ml/4 fl oz dry sherry
2 tbsp parsley – chopped
½ tsp Dijon mustard
1 tbsp red wine vinegar
small clove of garlic – crushed
4 tbsp olive oil

1. Put the leaves in a salad bowl.
2. Heat the oil in a small frying pan and cook the sausage over a medium heat until it begins to brown nicely.
3. Pour in the sherry and continue cooking until it burns off.
4. Scatter the parsley over.
5. Mix the last four ingredients into a dressing and pour over the salad and then add the sausage dice. Turn it all over carefully and serve.

Spinach Salad with Bacon and Avocado

Serves 4

This is quick, easy and delicious, and a touch tart. You could add some rocket, Treviso lettuce, dandelion leaves ("pissenlit" in French), or any other bitter salad you like.

4 handfuls spinach – washed and spun dry
225 g/8 oz smoked or green streaky bacon – diced
3 tbsp olive oil
handful of walnut pieces
2 ripe avocados – skinned and diced
4 tbsp red wine vinegar
2 tsp Dijon mustard
salt and pepper

1. Put the prepared spinach in a bowl.
2. Gently fry the bacon bits in the olive oil until they are well browned. At the same time carefully dry roast the walnut pieces in another pan.
3. Add the diced avocados to the spinach.
4. Remove the bacon with a slotted spoon and add to the spinach with the walnuts.
5. Add the vinegar to the oil and bacon fat and stir in. Add the mustard and stir in.
6. When nicely combined, pour the mixture over the spinach and gently toss the salad. Season to taste.

Tonno e Fagioli (Tuna and White Bean Salad)

Serves 4, 5 or 6

One of my all-time favourite salads, this is a good stand-by. There's usually a tin of tuna and bottle of white beans in the larder; then all you need is a small red onion, oil and vinegar. No cooking is involved and it's all ready in 15 minutes.

2 tins good tuna in olive oil – there should be enough, i.e. don't stint
2 tins/bottles (I prefer bottles) white beans (haricot blancs, cannellini)
3 tsp red wine vinegar
6 tbsp olive oil
salt and pepper
½ red onion – very thinly sliced
some chopped parsley if you have it

1. Drain the tuna. Drain and rinse the beans.
2. Whisk the vinegar, oil and salt and pepper into a vinaigrette.
3. Put the beans, tuna and onion into a bowl and pour over the sauce. Mix all the ingredients thoroughly, turning them over carefully. Taste and add more seasoning and more oil if necessary.
4. Sprinkle over the parsley.

Tuna Salad

Serves 4

Adapted from an early Nigel Slater recipe, this is very handy as a quick standby when you feel at a loss for something to serve as a light lunch.

2 x 200 g/7 oz tins of tuna – drained and flaked
2 tbsp Dijon mustard
4 tbsp tarragon vinegar
300 ml/10 fl oz/1¼ cups olive oil
4 tbsp low-fat yogurt – given the muslin or sieve treatment, i.e. drained a little, see page 64
2 tbsp parsley – finely chopped
2 tbsp chives – finely chopped
2 tbsp chervil – finely chopped (a plus if you can find it)
salt and pepper
½ cucumber – peeled, quartered, deseeded and finely chopped
2 spring onions – cleaned and finely chopped
1 tbsp sunflower seeds – lightly toasted
a little extra parsley – finely chopped

1. Put the tuna into a favourite serving bowl.
2. Whisk the mustard, vinegar, olive oil, yogurt, parsley, chives, chervil and salt and pepper together into a thick sauce.
3. Add the cucumber, onions and seeds.
4. Pour the sauce over the tuna and turn over all the ingredients carefully.
5. Sprinkle over the remaining parsley and serve with a crisp green lettuce.

A Mayonnaise-like Dressing

Not as soft and unctuous of course, but good with salmon, for instance, and asparagus, and does not involve the irksome though rewarding business of making mayonnaise! Heresy, I know...

1 tbsp cider vinegar
1 tsp Dijon mustard
juice of ¼ of a lemon
4–5 tbsp extra-virgin canola/colza oil

A Sauce for Asparagus and Artichokes

Serves 4

This recipe, based on one by Geraldine Holt, is a tasty change from the more traditional vinaigrettes to accompany welcome spring arrivals.

salt and pepper
1 tsp Dijon mustard
1 tsp white wine vinegar
4 tbsp olive oil
2 tbsp crème fraîche

1. Add a pinch of salt and pepper to a mixing bowl.
2. Mix in the mustard and vinegar.
3. Add the oil gently – stirring to emulsify.
4. Fold in the crème.
5. Taste for seasoning.

Everyday Vinaigrette

1 clove of garlic – pulped in a mortar with a pinch of salt
1 tbsp balsamic vinegar
1 tsp Dijon mustard
6 tbsp olive oil

1. Mix the first three ingredients thoroughly.
2. Add the olive oil and whisk to a viscous delight.

Or try this alternative:

3 tbsp olive oil
1 tbsp balsamic vinegar
juice of ½ lemon
salt
no mustard

Kara's Vinaigrette

1 clove of garlic
1 tsp Dijon mustard
1 tbsp cider vinegar
2 tbsp olive oil
2 tbsp walnut oil
salt and pepper

1. Pulp the garlic with salt.
2. Mix in the mustard and cider vinegar.
3. Whisk in the oils.
4. Test for seasoning.

Olive Oil and Lemon Juice Vinaigrette

A delicate sauce.

a pinch of salt
½ tsp Dijon mustard
juice of ½ lemon
3–4 tbsp olive oil

1. Mix the salt with the mustard and add in the lemon juice.
2. Add the olive oil and whisk.

4

Sauces

The thing about these sauces is that, apart from the Quick Tomato Sauce, none of them is cooked; each is assembled from high quality, fresh ingredients, and is designed to complement not overwhelm or mask.

Cucumber and Onion Raita

Serves 2 generously

A useful and tasty sauce for spicy dishes.

250 g/2 small pots yogurt – I use fat-free
¼ cucumber – peeled, quartered lengthwise, deseeded and
   grated
¼ red onion – grated
½ tsp garam masala
½ tsp chilli powder
salt to taste
mint or parsley – finely chopped

1. Whisk the yogurt smooth.
2. Add the cucumber, onion, garam masala, chilli, salt and chopped mint or parsley; mix thoroughly.
3. Chill if possible before using.

A Simple Sauce

Serves 4

For white fish – grilled or roasted. You could try adding some finely chopped mint leaves and a little very finely sliced garlic.

4 tbsp/80 ml/3 fl oz olive oil
juice of a lemon
salt and pepper

Whisk all the ingredients together.

Green Sauce

This is a stunner and goes well with salmon fillet or chicken. You need a decent pile of herbs. Use whatever is available with parsley, mint and chives as the base.

1 bunch parsley
1 bunch mint
2 bunches chives
1 bunch chervil/tarragon
1 tbsp capers
salt and pepper
2 cloves of garlic – sliced wafer-thin
1 tbsp Dijon mustard
2 lemons – juiced
200 ml/7 fl oz/¾ cup olive oil

1. Pile the herbs together and chop them roughly.
2. Add the capers, salt and garlic to the pile and chop thoroughly.
3. Put this in a bowl and mix in the mustard, lemon juice and the oil. Season with the pepper.
4. Taste it for the balance of lemon and olive oil; you should end up with a rough mush, a delicious-looking green mess!

Mint Sauce with Apple and Onion

This to my mind is so much nicer than traditional mint sauce. The apple and onion put a real spring in its step – helped on by the cider vinegar. Goes wonderfully with roast lamb or lamb chops.

leaves from a large bunch of mint
1 apple – peeled, cored and roughly chopped
1 small onion – quartered
salt
good splash of cider vinegar

1. Process the mint, apple and onion in a blender – not too finely; it should have texture.
2. Add some salt and a good splash of vinegar. Taste to see if it needs a little more of anything – it may take a couple of goes to get the balance right. Then leave to marinade in the fridge.
3. Bring it back to room temperature before serving.

Pesto Sauce

Pesto – the Italian name – Pistou – the French – is a basil-based sauce and a wonder for summer. Lovely and garlicky, it's a quick sauce for pasta or a sauce to spread on grilled vegetables; and it can be stirred into a soup of young vegetables. This recipe makes a decent amount.

100 g/4 oz basil leaves
4 cloves of garlic – crushed
25 g/1 oz pine nuts – optional
10 tbsp olive oil
salt and pepper
100 g/4 oz Parmesan cheese – grated

1. Put the basil, garlic and pine nuts in a processor. Whizz, adding the oil until you have a smoothish sauce. Season and transfer to a bowl.
2. Fold in the Parmesan and taste. Add more seasoning if you feel it needs it.

Quick Tomato Sauce

Adapted from the first *River Café Cook Book*, this is very useful for spreading on grilled aubergines or to accompany tuna, mackerel or salmon.

3 cloves of garlic – peeled and finely sliced
4 tbsp olive oil
2 x 800 g/28 oz tins tomatoes – drained of their juice
salt and pepper
handful fresh basil if you have some – chopped

1. Fry the garlic gently in 2 tablespoons of olive oil in a large pan but do not let it brown.
2. Add the broken up tomatoes, salt and pepper. Cook on a high heat, stirring frequently to prevent it burning, and watch out for splattering. Use the biggest wooden spoon you have. This will take about 20 minutes.
3. When little red pock marks appear, making it look as though the surface of the moon has turned red, you know it is almost there. It will have reduced considerably to a thick sauce with very little liquid left. Add the last two tablespoons of olive oil, and the basil, taste and check the seasoning.
4. To turn this into a coulis (puréed sauce), let it cool a little, then work it through a sieve. This takes a little time. Then reheat it. A tablespoonful on a plate looks like a deep red setting sun.

Tapenade

Serves 4

Based on Mireille Johnston's recipe – she got the mix just right – this is a traditional spread. The word originates from the Provençal for 'caper'. It's a great standby to have in the fridge and is simplicity itself to make.

You can serve it as a summer lunch on toast brushed with olive oil with a slice of the ripest tomato on top, or on grilled slices of courgettes or aubergines, or on savoury biscuits or small pieces of toast as an appetizer, or whatever! It is a favourite at St. Martin – and would even persuade Cal McCrae to come to lunch!

200 g/7 oz black olives – the oily fleshy Greek ones are best, carefully stoned; it's important to use the plumpest tastiest olives
6 anchovy fillets – chopped
2 tbsp capers
2 cloves of garlic – crushed
1 tsp fresh thyme
1 tbsp Dijon mustard
juice of a lemon
black pepper
120 ml/4 fl oz/½ cup olive oil

1. Put all the ingredients, except the oil, in a processor. Using the surge button, gradually pour in the oil, bringing it to a nice nobbly sludge, i.e. not too smooth.
2. Taste for balance; you may need a little more lemon juice. Pour into a bowl or plastic box, and dribble a little more olive oil over to form a preserving film. Keep in the fridge.

Tzatziki

This is adapted from Rena Salaman's lovely and authentic *Greek Food*. It's a refreshing garlicky sauce that goes particularly well with grilled summer vegetables, chicken and lamb.

500 ml/18 fl oz/2 cups low-fat organic yogurt – wrapped in muslin and squeezed gently to drain it a little or left overnight in a sieve to drain into a bowl
2 tbsp olive oil
2 tsp white wine or cider vinegar
2 cloves of garlic – pulped in a mortar with a little salt
2 fresh mint leaves – finely chopped
¼ medium cucumber – peeled, quartered lengthwise, deseeded and finely chopped
salt and pepper

1. Carefully scrape the drained yogurt into a mixing bowl.
2. In a separate small bowl, whisk the oil and the vinegar together. Mix in the garlic and the mint.
3. Fold this into the yogurt, then add the cucumber. Season lightly, taste and refrigerate.

Walnut and Garlic Sauce

For Magret de Canard. This is based on Jeanne Strang's recipe in *Goose Fat and Garlic*. It is a traditional sauce for duck breast – a constant favourite in south-west France, not a great place to be born a duck! It is very garlicky and quite wonderful. My wife Meredith described it as "mindboggling" on first tasting it, 20 years ago.

75 g/3 oz peeled walnuts – take care that bits of shell don't
   get included
50 g/2 oz garlic cloves – crushed
1 tbsp chopped parsley
salt and pepper – to taste
150 ml/5 fl oz /½ cup walnut oil

1. Put all the ingredients in a food mixer. Mix to a fairly fine texture. Add a little water if you need to.

5
Vegetables

Sonia Keitzs, an English neighbour, has green fingers and grows wonderful vegetables all year round. She often arrives with a bunch of something picked that morning, bursting out of its newspaper wrappings and demanding to be cooked forthwith. That is what is nice about cooking seasonally – the choice is often made for you. It is what is there – what looks good on the stand.

Here broad beans, asparagus, purple sprouting broccoli, spinach, courgettes, green beans, tomatoes, etc., all have their seasons and the wheel seems to turn at the moment you find yourself thinking, "I've had it with broccoli for a while!" One simple rule for vegetables – like fish – they must be fresh. Well, two rules – cook them until just soft to the bite, which means you must test them; so, easy-to-use kitchen tongs are an essential tool.

Broad Beans with Shallots and Bacon Bits

Serves 4

If they are really young you don't have to skin them – and, of course, you can use frozen. You could serve these topped with some tasty chèvre and olive oiled toast on the side as a starter or, if you add a green salad, you have lunch!

1 tbsp olive oil
100 g/4 oz streaky bacon – diced
2 small shallots – finely chopped
2 kg/4½ lb broad beans – shelled and skinned – an ideal task
  for guests who want to help
salt and pepper

1. Heat the oil in a medium pan. Gently fry the bacon, colouring it lightly.
2. Add the shallots and soften.
3. Add the brilliant green broad beans and 2 or 3 tablespoons of water. Season, remembering that the bacon may be salty.
4. Cover the pan and cook for 5–7 minutes; depending on the age of the beans they should be just tender.

Broccoli – Florence style

Serves 4

Many years ago I had lunch in a tiny workers' café in the centre of Florence – only open at midday. I watched the owner put down a plate of steaming broccoli – that was all there was on the plate – in front of a burly Italian and place a large jug of olive oil and salt and pepper beside it. The man poured on the oil and seasoned the irresistible plateful and ate it. That's simple eating. Of course, he may have had a veal chop after I left!

500 g/18 oz broccoli – stems stripped of rough outer layer and cut into bite-size pieces, florets cut likewise
olive oil
salt and pepper
lemon quarters

1. Steam the broccoli until tender but don't overcook it. Test it from time to time with the end of a sharp knife.
2. Transfer to a serving bowl and pour over the oil – be generous with it.
3. Season generously too and turn it all over carefully.
4. Serve with a small jug of olive oil on the table for those who are never satisfied and some lemon quarters.

Brussels Sprouts with Shallots

Serves 4

What to do with Brussels sprouts? This is a tasty option and quickly done. I favour the smaller ones, they are sweeter.

15 g/½ oz butter
1 tbsp olive oil
3 shallots – peeled and sliced
450 g/1 lb Brussels sprouts – outer leaves removed and halved
3 tbsp vegetable stock
salt and pepper

1. Melt the butter with the oil in a medium frying pan and gently sweat the shallots until soft.
2. Add the halved Brussels and turn with the shallots.
3. Cook for a couple of minutes before adding the stock. Turn again and season.
4. Cover and cook on a low heat until the Brussels are tender but not mushy. You want to retain some of their lovely green colour.

Cabbage with Capers and Balsamic Vinegar

Serves 4

Our English neighbour Julie Ide, herself an accomplished cook, put me onto Paola Gavin. This is based on the recipe in her excellent *Italian Vegetarian Cooking* and it's very tasty.

2 tbsp olive oil
1 small onion – chopped
1 green or Savoy cabbage – quartered, cored and shredded
2 tbsp hot water
1 tbsp capers – chopped if large
250 g/8 oz tinned tomatoes – put through a sieve
2 tbsp balsamic vinegar
salt and pepper

1. Heat the oil in a large saucepan and sweat the onion gently until opaque.
2. Add the cabbage and the water, and cook, covered, for 10 minutes, stirring from time to time.
3. Stir in the capers, tomato purée and the balsamic vinegar. Season well and cook, covered, until the cabbage is tender – about 30 minutes.

Cauliflower with Mustard Seeds and Fennel

Serves 4

Madhur Jaffrey, the Indian actress and cook, brings a touch of the sub-continent to the Mediterranean. This version of her recipe stands on its own and would be good served on the socca pancake (page 174) or with the "comfort" lentils (page 164), and is excellent as a vegetarian main course.

6 tbsp olive oil
1 tbsp black mustard seeds
2 tsp fennel seeds
3 cloves of garlic – finely chopped
¼ tsp turmeric
¼ tsp cayenne pepper
1 largish cauliflower – dismantled into small florets
4 tbsp hot water
salt to taste

1. Heat the oil in a large sauté pan. Put in the mustard and fennel seeds.
2. As soon as the mustard seeds begin to pop, add the garlic cloves. As they begin to turn colour, add the turmeric and cayenne and stir them in.
3. Add the cauliflower florets and turn them in the oily mixture. Add the water and turn the heat down.
4. Cook on a gentle heat, covered, for 20 minutes or until the cauliflower is just tender.
5. Uncover the pan and let any remaining water evaporate. Add salt to taste.

Courgettes with Garlic and Parsley

Serves 4

Tasty accompaniment to pretty much anything.

450 g/1 lb courgettes
salt and pepper
1 tbsp olive oil
1 tbsp chopped parsley
1 clove of garlic – finely chopped

1. Top and tail the courgettes. Peel them, leaving stripes of green. Cut them to index-finger thickness. Lightly salt them. Leave for a good hour in a colander/sieve so they lose their liquid. Shake them well and dry with kitchen paper.
2. Heat the oil in a large frying pan. Fry the rounds over a high heat so they colour lightly. Turn over with a pair of tongs or a spatula (depending on the amount of rounds you may have to repeat this).
3. Grind over lots of pepper. Throw over the parsley and garlic. Toss well. Turn down the heat to low, cover and cook for a few more minutes, being careful not to overcook them.

Gratin of Swiss Chard Stalks

Serves 4

Something to do with the stalks!

stalks from 1 kg/2¼ lb Swiss chard – cleaned up and cut into
  bite-size lengths
salt and pepper
2 tbsp Parmesan cheese – grated
olive oil

1. Heat the oven at 200°C/400°F/Gas Mark 6.
2. Soften the stalks in plenty of salted boiling water for 5 minutes. Drain thoroughly.
3. In a small oiled gratin dish, arrange a layer of the stalks and sprinkle a tablespoon of Parmesan over them, a little olive oil and season lightly. Repeat this until all the stalks are in the dish. Sprinkle over the remaining cheese and a little more oil.
4. Cook in the uppermost part of the oven for 15–20 minutes.
5. Finish it off with a minute under a hot grill.

Green Beans with Tomatoes

The fresher the beans and the riper the tomatoes, the better of course. Try this as a starter.

1 clove of garlic – thinly sliced
2 tbsp olive oil
250 g/½ lb cherry tomatoes – cut in half
salt and pepper
500 g/1 lb green beans

1. First make the sauce. Sauté the garlic lightly in the oil.
2. Add the tomatoes and cook for 10 minutes until the sauce looks unctuous but the tomatoes retain a bit of their shape. Add salt and pepper to taste.
3. Bring a pan of water to the boil and salt well. Add the beans and cook until tender – bite them to test them. Drain thoroughly and add to the sauce, turning them in it carefully.

Leeks in White Wine and Butter

Serves 4

Simple and delicious.

4 large leeks – just the white part – checked for residue, then cut
    into cork tube-shape
salt and pepper
glass of white wine
3 tbsp water
50 g/2 oz butter

1. Place the leek pieces in a shallow pan. Season with salt and pepper.
2. Pour in the wine and water, then add the butter. Put on the lid and bring up to a simmer. Cook over a low heat for about 20 minutes – the leeks should be beautifully tender.

Red Cabbage with Apple and Fresh Fruit Juices

Serves4+ depending on the size of the cabbage

This would be a good complement to some slow-fried sausages.

1 onion – chopped
1 tbsp olive oil
12 juniper berries – crushed
2 apples – peeled, cored and diced
1 stick of celery – chopped
1 red cabbage – cored, quartered and sliced
juice of 2 oranges and 2 lemons
1 tbsp wine vinegar
salt and pepper

1. Sweat the onion in the oil in a large saucepan until it softens.
2. Add the juniper berries and mix in.
3. Stir in the apple, celery and cabbage. Stir well and keep turning over gently for 5 minutes.
4. When the cabbage is starting to wilt, add the juices and the vinegar. Add some salt and cover the pan.
5. Cook for about 25 minutes when the cabbage should be a pinky red and soft. Add pepper and salt if needed.

Sautéed Mushrooms with Parsley and Garlic

Serves 4

Delicious as a vegetable side dish or on a slice of wholewheat toast as a snack or starter – with a poached egg on top?

4 tbsp olive oil
450 g/1 lb field mushrooms – sliced top to toe in thicknesses of 1cm/½ inch
1 clove of garlic – finely chopped
handful of parsley – chopped
salt and pepper

1. Heat the oil in a large frying pan. When hot, carefully put in the mushrooms. Turn them smartly in the oil – they'll soak it up quickly. After a couple of minutes when they're on their way, turn the heat down. Leave them to soften for about another 4 minutes – they will start to squeak and give off some liquid when you agitate them.
2. Turn up the heat and sprinkle the garlic and parsley over them. Turn them over in the pan and season.

Slow-Cooked Fennel with Garlic

Serves 4

Based on a recipe from Richard Olney's *Simple French Food*, this could serve as a vegetarian main course with some white beans or chickpeas. The slow initial cooking helps to caramelize the fennel lightly so it's worth taking the time.

2 large or 4 medium fennel bulbs – tough outer part removed, cleaned up and quartered or cut into eighths if the bulbs are very large
6 or more cloves of garlic – unpeeled, hooray!
3 tbsp olive oil
salt and pepper
6 tbsp water

1. Put the fennel and the garlic in a pan large enough to hold all the quarters in a single layer. Add the olive oil and a little salt.
2. Cook, uncovered, on a medium-low heat for 20 minutes, turning as the fennel colours. It should be nicely caramelized by the end.
3. Add the water, cover the pan and cook slowly until the fennel is super tender – about 30–40 minutes. The quarters should hold their shape and be infused with a deliciously mild taste of the garlic. Adjust the seasoning and serve.

Spicy Broccoli

Serves 4

My favourite way to eat broccoli is steamed with fruity olive oil and seasoning over it; but for a change you could try this spicy version.

450 g/1 lb broccoli – cut down to short stemmed florets
4–5 tbsp olive oil – depending on how juicy the lemons are
4 cloves of garlic – chopped
1 tsp cumin seeds
2–3 small red chillies – chopped, or a medium fresh green one
  – cored, deseeded and sliced
juice of 2 lemons

1. Steam the broccoli to just tender, then throw into a bowl of cold water, drain and set aside.
2. Heat the oil in a pan and gently soften the garlic.
3. Add the cumin seeds and the chillies. After half a minute add the lemon juice. Stir well and check the oil/lemon balance. Cook on for a couple of minutes to let the flavours meld.
4. Fold in the broccoli and turn it to reheat and soak up the sauce.

Swiss Chard Leaves in Garlicky Olive Oil

Serves 4

Spinach cooks well like this too.

1 kg/2¼ lb Swiss chard
4 tbsp olive oil
1 large clove of garlic – squashed
salt

1. Cut the leaves away from the stalks of the chard. (There is a delicious gratin for these stalks on page 74.) Soak and rinse them well. Shake off as much of the water as you can.
2. Heat the oil in a large saucepan or sauté pan. Put in the garlic and brown it over a moderate heat, taking care it doesn't burn.
3. Remove the garlic, add all the chard leaves and some salt, turning the leaves in the garlicky oil. Cover the pan and cook gently until the chard has collapsed and is a tender silky green marvel. Turn it over again and serve.

6
Vegetarian Dishes

These dishes are suitable as main courses for vegetarians but we ourselves often eat them as a light supper. Other options are in the Vegetables, Pasta, Light Lunches and Salads sections. Some vegetarians eat fish – which makes them non-meat eaters in my book rather than vegetarian, but it does make cooking for mixed company less complicated.

Caponata

This traditional Sicilian wonder, Jamie Oliver calls "incredible Sicilian Aubergine Stew". It's a good description. There are echoes of ratatouille, of course.

2 tbsp olive oil
2 large aubergines – cut in chunks, salted and left to drain, overnight if you can but at least an hour or two; they soak up less oil this way when cooked; dry them thoroughly
1 tsp dried oregano
1 small red onion – finely chopped
2 cloves of garlic – finely sliced
1 small bunch parsley – stalks chopped separately very finely (also chop the leaves finely to scatter over the finished dish)
handful of green olives – stoned if you have time
2 tbsp capers
2–3 tbsp herb vinegar (I use tarragon vinegar), not more or it dominates
5 ripe tomatoes (or tinned if it's not the season) – roughly chopped
salt and pepper

1. Heat the olive oil in a large pan. Add the aubergines and oregano. Cook on the highest heat to brown the chunks, turning them as they colour. This is the longest part of the cooking, as you may have to do this in a couple of stages.
2. When the aubergines are nicely coloured, add the onion, garlic and the parsley stalks. Cook for a couple of minutes. Add a little more olive oil if you feel it needs it.
3. Add the olives, capers and herb vinegar.
4. When the vinegar has evaporated, add the tomatoes, bring back to simmer and cook for 15–20 minutes until the aubergines feel really melting.
5. Season with pepper and salt – bearing in mind that you salted the aubergines earlier.
6. Sprinkle over the parsley. Serve with extra olive oil on hand.

Chickpeas with Tomato Sauce and Spinach

Serves 6-8

This is based on a *River Café Cook Book* recipe and is a handy dish as a vegetarian main course – but lovely with grilled/fried sausages too!

2 tbsp Quick Tomato Sauce (page 62)

5 tbsp olive oil

1 fennel bulb – chopped into small dice

1 red onion – chopped small

large stick of celery – chopped into small dice

2 dried chillies

salt and pepper

250 ml/8 fl oz/1 cup white wine

900 g/32 oz tinned chickpeas – drained and rinsed

500 g/1 lb 4 oz spinach or Swiss chard leaves – thoroughly washed and spun dry

3 tbsp chopped parsley

more olive oil

juice of ½ lemon

1. Make the tomato sauce. Heat the olive oil in a large sauté pan. Add the fennel, onion and celery, and soften for about 20 minutes.
2. Add the chillies and season well.
3. Add the wine and reduce down until just the oil remains.
4. Add the tomato sauce and cook gently for 10 minutes.
5. Add the chickpeas and the spinach or Swiss chard leaves, and turn in carefully. You can add the spinach in handfuls – covering the pan for a minute each time, it will spill but it's satisfying to see it gradually wilt and become part of the dish when it's thoroughly heated through.
6. Fold in the parsley, sprinkle over a little more olive oil and the lemon juice.

Courgette and Tomato Tian/Tortino

Serves 4

This traditional summer dish is adapted from two fabulous sources – Elizabeth David and Anna del Conte. For lunch or supper, you just need a crisp green salad to accompany it.

3 or 4 medium courgettes – sliced very thinly
2 tbsp olive oil
2 onions – chopped
2 cloves of garlic – thinly sliced
2 tbsp chopped parsley
250 g/8 oz tomatoes – fresh if good enough, otherwise tinned, drained and chopped
salt and pepper
1 tsp dried oregano
3 tbsp grated Parmesan cheese
3 tbsp breadcrumbs – wholewheat or 100 per cent rye
extra olive oil

1. Lightly salt the courgettes and leave them to drain in a colander for an hour, then dry them thoroughly with kitchen paper or clean tea towel. It helps to prepare them in advance.
2. Heat the olive oil in a large pan and fry the onions gently until they are pale golden and tinged with brown – about 15 minutes.
3. Stir in the garlic and parsley and let them cook gently for a couple of minutes.

4. Fold in the tomatoes and mix well. Let them cook together on a low heat for a good 10 minutes. (Elizabeth David makes the case for cooking the tomatoes beforehand – thus concentrating their taste – and mixing them into the courgettes just before the baking stage.)
5. Add the courgettes and turn them into the mixture. Cook, covered, for 15 minutes – until the courgettes begin to soften and become opaque.
6. Heat the oven at 200°C/400°F/Gas Mark 6.
7. Uncover the pan and continue cooking for another 10 minutes. It's important that the mixture is not watery.
8. Season with salt, pepper and the oregano. Mix in the seasoning well and taste.
9. Brush a suitably sized and presentable shallow oven dish with oil and turn the mix into it.
10. Mix the cheese and the breadcrumbs and sprinkle these over the tian. Trickle some olive oil in a filigree pattern over the top and bake for about 15–20 minutes – it should come out nicely browned and sizzling.

Courgette Fritters

This is adapted from Jojo Tulloh's *Freshly Picked – Kitchen Garden Cooking in the City* and is handy for vegetarians – when others are having fishcakes perhaps. It's important to check the seasoning for depth, as you assemble the mixture. Tzatziki (page 64) on the side is recommended.

3 medium courgettes – scrubbed and dried
2 large bulbed spring onions – cleaned and grated
1 clove of garlic – finely chopped
zest of a lemon
1 tbsp chickpea flour
1 tbsp chopped herbs – mint, parsley, chives
salt and pepper
2 eggs – beaten
2 tbsp olive oil

1. Grate the courgettes into a colander. Salt them lightly and leave for at least an hour to drain. Squeeze out the remaining liquid. It's important to take the time for this, especially when the courgettes are young and fresh, otherwise the mixture will be too watery.

2. Put the rest of the ingredients, except the eggs and the olive oil, in a mixing bowl and add the courgettes. Season well, bearing in mind you have already salted the courgettes. Combine everything thoroughly, then check the seasoning.

3. Add the whisked eggs and mix in.

4. Heat a tablespoon of olive oil in a large frying pan. Scoop up a dessertspoonful of the mixture and drop it into the pan. Press it down with the flat of the spoon. Repeat the process but don't overcrowd the pan.

5. Cook over a medium to hot heat quite quickly but be careful not to burn them. Take a peek with a spatula, then flip them over after a couple of minutes. Check that they are cooked through and serve.

Mellanzane Parmigiana (Aubergine in Tomato Sauce with Parmesan)

Serves 4

This is a traditional dish that shows up all over Italy, though it signals "the south" to me. Speculation about the origin of its name ranges from "parmigiana" being the Sicilian word for the slats of a shutter – i.e. a dish of layers – to parmigiano reggiano (the cheese) which features in every layer. It can be served as a starter (cut the aubergines into rounds and follow the same steps below but build individual round pyramids on a small bed of mixed leaves, dressed as you like) or a main course for a light lunch or supper. Or you could serve it with roast chicken or meat – sausages for instance.

2 medium aubergines – sliced carefully lengthwise, roughly 0.5cm/¼ inch thick – watch out for fingers!
salt and pepper
Quick Tomato Sauce – see page 62
olive oil
Parmesan cheese

1. Salt the aubergine slices and leave in a colander over a bowl for a couple of hours to draw out the liquid. Put slices between sheets of kitchen paper to dry them thoroughly. Meanwhile make the tomato sauce.
2. Heat the oven at 200°C/400°F/Gas Mark 6.

3. Heat the grill to very hot. Brush the aubergine slices lightly with olive oil on one side. Place on the grill oiled side down. Brush the exposed side with oil. A pair of tongs is useful here. Check that the slices are cooking and after 3 or 4 minutes turn them over and cook for a further 3 or 4 minutes. Turn them back again if you like – the point is that both sides should be nicely charred and soft; undercooked aubergine is uneatable.

4. Lightly oil the bottom of a baking dish – the one from which you are going to serve the aubergines – then cover with a layer of tomato sauce, followed by a layer of aubergines, topped by a sprinkling of Parmesan. Salt and pepper lightly each stage. Repeat this process until you've used all the ingredients. Sprinkle the last layer of aubergines with a good covering of Parmesan.

5. Put the dish in the top part of the oven for about 20 minutes – checking a couple of times to make sure it's not burning. Then let it rest for a bit – it's best served tepid.

Courgette Muffins

Serves 6 as a starter

Our friend Fronza Woods, who is vegetarian and cooks delicious delicacies, introduced us to these little numbers. They serve as a vegetable or as a starter with a tomato coulis.

2 courgettes – unpeeled and grated
2 tbsp Emmental cheese – grated
4 tbsp onion – grated
1 tbsp fine breadcrumbs – wholewheat or rye
salt and pepper
2 eggs

1. Heat the oven at 200°C/400°F/Gas Mark 6.
2. Combine the first four ingredients, season well and mix thoroughly.
3. Check the seasoning and fold in the eggs.
4. Oil the muffin cups. This amount is enough to fill one of those rubber trays of twelve. Fill each cup with the mixture and carefully transfer to the middle of the oven. Bake for 30–40 minutes. They should be springy and nicely brown. Serve in a tablespoon of tomato coulis.

Red Peppers Stuffed with Tomato and Chèvre

Serves 4

This is a useful and reliable dish – as a starter or light lunch with a green salad. A single half pepper may be enough to serve per person as a starter.

4 red peppers – choose ones that will balance well when halved
8 medium ripe tomatoes or tinned ones – quartered
4 cloves of garlic – finely sliced
2 round fresh chèvre – as fresh as you can find – cut in half
8 tbsp olive oil
salt and pepper
extra olive oil
8 basil leaves – optional but nice

1. Heat the oven at 200°C/400°F/Gas Mark 6.
2. Cut the peppers in half lengthwise through the stem, and cut out the white stem base and the seeds.
3. Put a quartered tomato and some sliced garlic in each half pepper. Tuck half a chèvre in each. Dribble a tablespoon of olive oil over each half and season with salt and pepper.
4. Cover a shallow oven pan with foil and brush it with oil. Place the pepper halves carefully on the tray, cook them in the upper part of the oven for about 40 minutes - 1 hour; the time depends on the size and thickness of the peppers, but they should be very tender and oozing with the sweet juices of the tomatoes and peppers when you check for doneness at about 30 minutes.
5. Put a basil leaf on each. They are best served tepid.

7

Fish

Fish has to be super fresh; a mushy mackerel is a waste of time and will put people off fish, as overcooked cabbage and broccoli put generations of school kids off vegetables. If the fish is fresh, it needs very little help – there are two or three simple sauces in this section that complement rather than mask and are worth offering up.

Baked Mackerel Fillets

Serves 4

This recipe is adapted from *Marcella's Kitchen* (Marcella Hazan, of course), a book well worth seeking out. It makes a good lunch or light supper. A plate of green beans, dressed with olive oil and salt and/or some lovely ripe tomatoes, sliced and similarly dressed, would go beautifully with this very tasty dish. You can use the same stuffing on butterflied sardines – they would need only a bare 5 minutes at 180°C/350°F/Gas Mark 4.

4 mackerel – very fresh (essential with mackerel) in fillets and skin removed (ask your fishmonger to do this)

Stuffing
3 tbsp chopped parsley
1 clove of garlic – chopped
3 anchovy fillets – chopped
3 tbsp capers – chopped
5 tbsp wholewheat breadcrumbs
3 tbsp olive oil
salt and pepper

1. Heat the oven at 200°C/400°F/Gas Mark 6.
2. Reserve one tablespoon each of the olive oil and breadcrumbs. Mix the remaining stuffing ingredients thoroughly in a bowl.
3. Wash and pat the fish dry, removing any lingering bones.
4. Line a shallow baking tray with some foil and brush with oil to prevent the fillets sticking. Lay half the fillets "skin" side down and spoon over half the stuffing. Cover each with a second fillet and spoon over what's left of the stuffing. Sprinkle with the remaining breadcrumbs and olive oil (more oil if you think it needs it).
5. Bake in the top part of the oven for 15 minutes or more, depending on the thickness of the fillets. They should come out sizzling and the breadcrumbs crispy on top – but be careful not to overcook them.
6. A ripe tomato salad is a good counter to the richness of the mackerel.

Blackened Salmon with Orange Yogurt Sauce

Serves 4

A very good dish for company, this is easily adapted to feed more than four. Allow 200 g/7 oz of salmon fillet per person.

800 g/28 oz salmon fillet – skin and small bones removed
2 tbsp olive oil
more olive oil for sautéing

For the Orange Yogurt Sauce
4 tbsp/80 ml/3 fl oz olive oil
400 ml/14 fl oz/1½ cups yogurt of choice – whisked smooth
zest and juice of 1 large juicy orange

For the Herb and Spice Mix
3 tsp dried thyme, dried rosemary, dried oregano
3 tsp dry roasted cumin seeds – roughly ground
1½ tsp Spanish sweet smoked paprika, cayenne pepper
3 cloves of garlic – pulped in a mortar with a pinch of salt
3 tsp salt – ground fine if sea salt is used

1. Make the sauce by whisking the olive oil into the yogurt, followed by the zest and juice of the orange. Set it aside.
2. Put all the herbs and spices in a bowl and mix them thoroughly.
3. Run your fingers over the top of the fillets to check that all the small bones have been removed. Cut up the salmon into squares roughly 3 cm/1$\frac{1}{2}$ inch in size – they need to be cooked quite quickly so mustn't be too large. Put them in a bowl and add the olive oil. Turn the salmon carefully until it is well covered.
4. Tip the salmon into the bowl with the herb and spice mix. Again turn the salmon carefully until all the pieces are well covered in the mix.
5. Pour a couple of tablespoons of oil into a large frying pan. When hot, transfer the "blackened" salmon to the pan and fry for 4–5 minutes. Check for doneness, try not to overcook; it's better that some pieces are slightly underdone – they continue to cook a bit off the heat.
6. Serve over a steaming dish of brown basmati rice. Don't forget the sauce!

Rich Squid Stew

This recipe, based on one by Valentina Harris, gives the squid time to soften up in the unctuous tomatoey sauce.

1 small onion – finely chopped
1 clove of garlic – finely chopped
5 tbsp olive oil
450 g/1 lb prepared and cleaned squid – from about
    750 g/1¼ lb unprepared, tentacles and wings included –
    sliced into ribbons lengthwise
good handful of parsley – finely chopped
6 tbsp white wine
3 tbsp tomato concentrate
4 tbsp vegetable/fish stock
salt and pepper

1. Gently fry the onion and garlic in the oil until soft but uncoloured.
2. Add the squid and parsley and turn them over in the onion and oil. Cook for about 7-8 minutes until the squid is nicely opaque.
3. Add the wine and let it bubble away for about 3 minutes.
4. Stir in the tomato concentrate and add the stock. Cover and cook for 30 minutes.
5. Season well and serve over basmati rice.

Mackerel Escabeche

*Serves 10-20 depending on the size of the fish
and what else there'll be to eat*

Green beans go well with the mackerel or just a green salad.

10 whole mackerel – filleted and checked for bones, ask the
fishmonger the day before you collect to do this
flour – seasoned with salt and pepper
500 ml/18 fl oz/2 cups olive oil
500 ml/18 fl oz/2 cups white wine vinegar
250 ml/9 fl oz/1 cup water
3 heads of garlic – cloves separated and peeled
6 bay leaves
a few thyme branches

1. Slice the fillets in four. Dip them in the flour and shake off the excess.
2. Heat 6 tablespoons/125 ml oil in a large frying pan. Fry the fillets for a couple of minutes each side – just enough to colour them. Drain them on kitchen paper. Put them in a pretty bowl.
3. Put the rest of the ingredients – including the remaining oil – in a saucepan and bring gently to the boil. Pour this mixture over the fillets.
4. Refrigerate overnight or longer and serve at room temperature with the marinade.

Spicy Mussels with a Soupy Sauce

Serves 4

This is based on a recipe by Marcella Hazan and is a regular lunch dish here. It's simple and satisfying.

The best mussels are called bouchot. The word describes the method of cultivation – i.e. on a pole stuck in the estuary. They are not huge but are *plein* (full) and yellow when cooked. The amount of mussels I recommend using in this recipe is generous and will probably serve 6, but they are delicious so who knows!

2 large cloves of garlic – chopped
6 tbsp olive oil
2 tbsp chopped parsley
2–3 dry chillies, more or less to taste – deseeded and chopped
300 g/12 oz tinned (or fresh) tomatoes – drained and chopped
2 kg/4½ lb mussels – cleaned (i.e. beardless and scraped free of any gunge)
4 slices of wholewheat bread – toasted and rubbed with a bruised clove of garlic

1. In a large casserole sauté the garlic in the oil until it colours.
2. Add the parsley and chillies. Stir a couple of times.
3. Add the tomatoes. Cook for about 25 minutes over a moderate heat, stirring from time to time.
4. When the sauce is ready, put in the mussels and, with a spoon, turn them over carefully in the sauce. Cover and turn up the heat to high. Give the casserole a shake, gripping the top with your thumbs, or stir the mussels again in the sauce. They will take about 5 minutes to cook through. They are ready when they have opened up well.
5. Toast the bread and rub with the bruised garlic clove. Pile the steaming mussels on the toast.

Fish Curry

Serves 4

This is adapted from Nigel Slater's recipe. It's a good dish for company – allow 150 g/5 oz of fish per person. You can make the basic sauce earlier or even the night before and prepare the fish pieces too. Then all you have to do is reheat the curry sauce and slip in the fish in the appropriate order while you cook some basmati rice. Can also be served with cucumber raita or a fresh chutney.

2 medium onions – chopped
2 cloves of garlic – chopped
1 tbsp olive oil
1 tsp black mustard seeds
a thumbnail size piece of fresh ginger – chopped
3 small red chillies (the heat level is a matter of taste) – chopped
1 tsp each garam masala, cayenne, turmeric
225 g/8 oz fresh or tinned tomatoes – chopped
500 ml/1 pint/2 cups stock
250 g/9 oz mussels
8 clams – if you can find them
600 g/20 oz white fish in fillets – this could be monkfish, haddock, cod or some of each, preferably fish that holds its shape when cooked in pieces
8 prawns in their shells
1 tbsp yogurt – whisked smooth
salt
a handful of chopped parsley for sprinkling over the dish

1. In a casserole large enough to hold all the fish, fry the chopped onions and the garlic gently in the oil until soft.
2. Add the mustard seeds and ginger and mix.
3. Add the chopped chilli and mix.
4. Add the garam masala, cayenne and turmeric and mix.
5. Add the chopped tomatoes and let them mingle with the spices for 5 minutes.
6. Add the stock and bring everything to the boil.
7. Let this sauce simmer for 15 minutes.
8. Clean the mussels (see page 104). Scrub the clams if you have them. Check the fish fillets for bones and cut into bite-size pieces. Have the prawns standing by.
9. Stir in the yogurt carefully. Reheat the sauce if you have precooked it.
10. Slip in the white fish and cook until it turns opaque.
11. Then add the mussels, clams and prawns. Cook gently, making sure that the sauce is covering the fish, until the mussels and clams open and the prawns heat through. (I sometimes throw the mussels and clams in a saucepan with a tablespoon of water to get them to open, then add them to the curry.)
12. Check the salt, add the parsley and bring this bubbling colourful wonder to the table.

Salmon Fishcakes

Serves 2

Another recipe based on a Nigel Slater recipe. I have always loved fishcakes – must be the comfort food factor kicking in – but these days of course the fact they usually contain 50 per cent potato causes trouble for me as a diabetic. This recipe solves the problem by leaving the potato out! The dill and the grain mustard make the fishcakes special and they sometimes serve as a tasty starter. If you keep them small and cook them quickly, they'll be crisp and brown on the outside and still succulent inside.

Yogurt sauce
2 x 125 ml pots low-fat yogurt
1 tsp grain mustard
good pinch of chopped dill (from the main bunch)
salt

The Fishcakes
400 g/1 lb salmon fillet – skinless and checked for bones
white of an egg
1 tbsp chickpea flour – of course, plain flour works as well
1 tsp grain mustard
juice of ½ lemon
bunch of dill – chopped fine
salt and pepper
2 tbsp olive oil

1. Mix all the yogurt sauce ingredients and refrigerate until you are ready to eat.
2. Cut up the salmon fillets in roughly equal-size pieces. Put these in a mixer and pulse three or four times. Avoid working them too much and producing slush at the end. You could just cut them up in small pieces if this suits better.
3. Put the salmon in a bowl. Turn in the egg white and the flour, and then the mustard, lemon juice, and the dill. Season with salt and pepper.
4. It's a good idea to taste the mix for seasoning at this point – the dill and the salt should come through.
5. Refrigerate if not using immediately.
6. Heat the oil in a frying pan and using a dessertspoon scoop out a dollop and make a ball. Put this in the pan and flatten it gently. Cook on a medium-high flame, crisping and browning the outside while making sure the interior cooks through.
7. Serve with a fennel salad (page 43) and the mustardy yogurt dipping sauce on the side.

Fish in Tomato and White Wine Sauce

Serves 4

As always, use very fresh fish. You can make the sauce beforehand and add the fish 10 minutes before serving. This dish is very comforting on a rainy day. Swiss chard or spinach goes well with it or you could simply serve rice.

4 tbsp olive oil
1 small onion – chopped
2 cloves of garlic – chopped
2 tbsp chopped parsley
8 tbsp white wine
200 g/8 oz tinned tomatoes and their juice – broken up
900 g/2 lb white fish fillet – hake, haddock, cod are good choices – washed and patted dry
salt and pepper

To make the sauce:

1. Heat the oil in a pan large enough to take all the fish in a single layer. Add the onion and garlic, and cook gently until the onion is soft and the garlic begins to colour.
2. Add the parsley and stir in.
3. Turn up the heat and add the wine – let it bubble for a minute or so. Add the tomatoes and fold in.
4. Turn the heat down and, stirring occasionally, cook gently for 20 minutes. Season and taste.

5. When you are ready to use the sauce, bring the sauce up to simmer and season the fish. Add to the sauce and cook gently for 5 minutes.
6. Turn over carefully and cook for a further 5 minutes.

Simple Sea Bass

Serves 4

This dish, and the Simple Salmon Fillet, are based on recipes from an article I cut out from a newspaper ages ago by Quentin Blake, the illustrator. You can cook sea bream in the same way, though you might need two to make up the weight, and these won't need to be cooked as long – perhaps 15–20 minutes. I recently used rosemary instead of thyme, which worked well.

1 x 1 kg 200 g/2½ lb bass – scales left on
salt and pepper
large bunch thyme
The Simple Sauce on page 58

1. Heat the oven at 240°C/475°F/Gas Mark 9.
2. Wash and dry the fish, being careful not to remove the scales. Salt the inside of the fish and stuff with sprigs of thyme.
3. Lay the fish on the remaining thyme in an oven tray and add salt and pepper. Cook for 25 minutes, adjusting the time to suit the fish as necessary.
4. Peel back the hardened skin to release the beautifully cooked fillets. This is a bit tricky but worth taking time over.
5. Serve with green beans or the courgettes on page 73 or a green salad, and the Simple Sauce.

Simple Salmon Fillet (1)

Serves 4

See Simple Sea Bass for the origin of this succulent slow way of cooking a fillet of salmon. The Green Sauce on page 59 goes wonderfully with both versions.

**4 fillets of salmon – skin left on and weighing about
    180–200 g/6–7 oz each**
salt and pepper

1. Run your finger over the surface of the fillets to check for bones. Wash the fillets and pat dry. Place them in a sauté pan skin side down.
2. Without any oil added to the pan, cook them over the lowest possible heat for about 20 minutes or until you see the lower half becoming opaque.
3. Season with salt and pepper and cover the pan. Continue cooking until the creamy white juice forms on the surface of the fillets, indicating that they are done. The whole process can take 30 minutes, depending on the thickness of the fillets – it's the slow cooking that produces the wonderful result.

Simple Salmon Fillet (2)

Serves as many people as you have fillets!

I include this because it is easy and quick to do for company – a fillet a person.

Swiss chard or spinach goes well and lends a lovely contrast in colour.

Fillets of salmon – skin left on, checked for bones, washed and patted dry
salt and pepper
lemon wedges

1. Heat the oven at 140°C/275°F/Gas Mark 1.
2. Cover the bottom of a shallow roasting tin with foil. Oil it lightly. Place the fillets on it. Salt and pepper them. Put them on the middle shelf of the oven for 15 minutes; as in the previous recipe, the white juices indicate doneness.
3. Serve with lemon wedges.

Spicy Courgettes and Prawns with Fresh Coriander

Serves 4

The ingredients for this recipe, adapted from one by Madhur Jaffrey, take a little time to get ready – but then it takes no time to cook and is deliciously rewarding. Serve over brown basmati rice.

450 g/1 lb courgettes – topped and tailed
450 g/1 lb unshelled or good quality shelled prawns
1½ tsp cumin seeds – finely ground
½ tsp turmeric
½ tsp chilli powder or cayenne
1 fresh green chilli – deseeded and chopped
1 tsp grated fresh ginger
1 good tsp salt plus extra for sprinkling on the courgettes
1 tbsp lemon juice
3 tinned tomatoes – broken up with some juice (115 ml/
    4 fl oz)
2–3 extra tbsp water
5 tbsp olive oil
6 cloves of garlic – finely chopped
75 g/3 oz fresh coriander – hard stems removed, leaves
    chopped

1. Run your vegetable parer down the courgettes to make a striped pattern. Halve them and cut them in thin strips so that they cook in no time. If the strips look too long, halve them again. Put them in a colander or sieve and salt them lightly. Set them over a bowl for an hour to drain.
2. Shell the prawns if necessary and put them back in the fridge.
3. In a small bowl, put the cumin, turmeric, chilli powder or cayenne, green chilli, ginger and salt. Add the lemon juice, tomatoes with their juice, and the extra water.
4. Pat the courgettes dry. Retrieve the prawns from the fridge.
5. Heat the oil in a large frying pan with a lid. When it's hot, put in the garlic. As it colours, put in the ingredients from the bowl, the courgettes and the coriander. Turn them carefully and over a gentle heat bring the pan up to a simmer.
6. Add the prawns and cover the pan. Cook for roughly 5 minutes to allow the courgettes to soften and the prawns to heat through.

8
Chicken

Chicken is versatile; it is readily available, the ways to cook it are legion, and it is reasonably priced; it is also a healthy option and, as Jamie Oliver says of his way of roasting – it is simply delicious. Guinea fowl and quail are easy to find now and fun to try too.

Charlotte's Chicken Tagine

Serves 4; for 6 or 8 add a few extra pieces

Our friend Charlotte Fraser – a wonderful cook and author of *Flavours of the Sun* – put me on to this and it has been very useful. It's spicy and delicious and a good dish for company because it gently gets on with cooking itself, and needs only rice as accompaniment.

1 large chicken – jointed in 8–10 pieces
3 onions – peeled and quartered
2 medium fennel bulbs – outer leaves cut off, cored and
   quartered
6 cloves of garlic – chopped
1 tsp each turmeric, cumin, paprika, cayenne and ground
   ginger
1 tsp saffron threads
salt and pepper
228 ml/8 fl oz/1 cup vegetable stock
olive oil
good handful green olives
1 preserved lemon – rind only, cut in strips
2 tbsp chopped coriander or parsley

1. Put the chicken pieces in a casserole or, even better, a tagine if you have one.
2. Pack in the onions and fennel pieces.
3. Sprinkle over the garlic and spices. Season with salt and pepper.
4. Pour over the stock and drizzle over some olive oil.
5. Bring to a very gentle simmer. Carefully turn over the contents in the liquid. Put the lid on and cook for 1 hour, basting occasionally. The chicken pieces should be sumptuously meltingly collapsed when ready.
6. Add the olives and lemon rind and continue cooking for 10–15 minutes more.
7. Add the coriander or parsley just before serving with a steaming plate of brown basmati rice.

Chicken Breasts with Caper and Lemony Sauce

Serves 4

This is a lazy supper or lunch and no less delicious for that. The trick, if you can call it that, is to cook them very gently – then they don't dry out. Sautéed spinach or Swiss chard goes well with this and perhaps half a baked sweet potato – the colour scheme is inviting.

4 free-range or organic chicken breasts
2 tbsp flour – I use chickpea – seasoned with salt and pepper
4 tbsp olive oil or 50 g/2 oz butter – I prefer oil
1 lemon – zest and juice
2 tbsp capers – chopped

1. Drag the chicken pieces in the well-seasoned flour, pressing them down so they get a good dusting. Shake off the excess.
2. Heat the fat or oil in a medium frying pan – large enough to hold the chicken in one layer. When hot, slip in the breasts. Turn the heat to low and cook for 15 minutes or so, turning them once or twice, until just past the pink stage; you can cut carefully into the thickest part of the chicken to test. Transfer the chicken to warm plates.
3. Add the lemon juice, zest and capers to the pan and season. Cook gently for a minute, stir and taste for perfection. Spoon some sauce over each serving of chicken.

Chicken Breasts in a Spicy Lemon and Parsley Sauce

Serves 4

A tasty eastern take on gently sautéed chicken breasts.

1 largish onion – chopped
1 cinnamon stick – broken up
4 tbsp olive oil
4 chicken breasts – spliced in half lengthways
juice of 2 lemons
salt and pepper
2 tbsp parsley – chopped
2–3 small red chillies – chopped

1. Cook the onion with the cinnamon gently in the oil until soft.
2. Add the chicken breasts with the lemon juice, and season with salt and pepper. Turn them over after 3 minutes and cook for a further 3 minutes.
3. Add the parsley and the chillies. Turn the breasts in the sauce and continue cooking for a further 5 minutes. The exact cooking time depends on the thickness of the breasts. Cut into the thickest part of one to check: if it is still very pink, continue to cook for another couple of minutes.

Chicken Fricassée with Red Wine Vinegar

Serves 4

This is another recipe adapted from one by Marcella Hazan. It makes a delicious lunch or dinner dish for guests, and is very simple to make. Serve with leeks in butter and white wine and brown basmati rice.

8 chicken pieces – legs, thighs, wings and breasts – the choice is yours!
3 tbsp vegetable oil for sautéing
chickpea flour – seasoned with salt and pepper
4 anchovy fillets – finely chopped
large clove of garlic – finely chopped
1 tsp chopped fresh rosemary – finely chopped
2 tbsp olive oil
6 tbsp red wine vinegar

1. Wash the chicken pieces, then dry them well.
2. Heat the vegetable oil in a sauté pan, large enough to accommodate the chicken in a single layer.
3. Turn the chicken pieces in the flour and shake off the excess.

4. Slip them in the pan. Sauté for 5 minutes on a medium heat, turning them as they colour up. Remove them to a plate and set aside. Pour off the oil and clean the pan – taking care not to burn yourself.
5. Combine the chopped anchovies, garlic and rosemary.
6. Heat the olive oil in the cleaned pan. Put in the chopped ingredients, this time over a low heat. Cook for a couple of minutes until that lovely garlic smell rises, stirring often. Carefully return the chicken pieces to the pan and turn them in the oil. Raise the heat and add the vinegar, turning the chicken again. Let the vapour from the vinegar evaporate and then lower the heat and cover the pan. Allow about 30–40 minutes to cook the chicken to tenderness. Add a little water to the pan if you see it drying out.

Chicken Wings Roasted with Lemon and Black Pepper

Serves 4

This is based on Nigel Slater's answer to Colonel Sanders and is the real deal on truly fingerlickin' good. An ideal TV-watching supper – with a green sauce perhaps.

Let's say 5 each = 20 free-range chicken wings
2 lemons, halved for juicing
1½ tbsp black peppercorns
3 tbsp olive oil
a few bay leaves
sea salt

1. Heat the oven at 180°C/350°F/Gas Mark 4.
2. Put the chicken wings in a large bowl and squeeze the lemon juice over them.
3. Pound the peppercorns in a mortar or grind them mechanically – they should not go to powder. Mix the pepper with the oil and pour over the wings, turning them over thoroughly. Cut up the lemon shells.

4. Spread some foil over a shallow oven tray, large enough to hold the wings in a single layer and brush with olive oil.

5. Put the wings in the tray and distribute the cut-up lemon shells and the bay leaves round them. Scatter sea salt over the tray.

6. Roast for about 45 minutes, turning once. Then increase the heat to 200°C/400°F/Gas Mark 6 and roast for 5 more minutes.

7. Eat slowly, licking your fingers often! A finger bowl per person would be polite too.

Chicken with 40 Cloves of Garlic

Serves 4

This is a traditional recipe from south-west France, and particularly good with the pink-sheathed garlic grown all round us. The bird sits on the garlic for a couple of hours, and hatches a beautiful dish. It also can't fail to be a conversation piece – as people may feel nervous about those 40 cloves of garlic! They have little to fear; it is soft and sweet after the cooking. Serve with some brown basmati rice perhaps, a salad or green vegetable.

1 chicken – washed and thoroughly dried
salt and pepper
3 tbsp olive oil
about 40 large garlic cloves (new season garlic is best) – left unpeeled
2 fennel bulbs – outer leaves removed and halved
sprigs of rosemary, sage, parsley, thyme and a couple of bay leaves
½ small wine glass of white wine
1 tbsp chickpea flour

1. Heat the oven at 190°C/375°F/Gas Mark 5.
2. Season the chicken well with salt and pepper. Gently brown it in a tablespoon of olive oil in a large sauté pan. Remove the chicken to a plate.
3. Put the garlic and all the remaining ingredients except the wine and the flour in a casserole, add two tablespoons of olive oil and turn everything thoroughly in it.

4. Place the chicken on top and dribble over it some more olive oil, and an extra sprinkling of salt.
5. Make a paste with a spoonful of flour and some water. Carefully spread the paste round the rim of the lid of the casserole – this seals it. Cook in the oven.
6. After 2 hours' cooking, gingerly lift the lid and remove the chicken and the meltingly soft garlic to a serving platter.
7. Spoon off all but a tablespoon of the oil and deglaze the casserole with the white wine. Reduce this sauce a little and transfer it to a small jug.

Grilled Strips of Magret (Duck Breast)

Serves 2

This is a very quick way to do magret; it's important not to overcook the strips. The sauce is the thing though – upstages the duck every time! Serve with green beans perhaps.

1 magret – some of the fat trimmed and cut into "thick middle finger" wide strips lengthwise
salt and pepper
½ the amount of Walnut and Garlic sauce, page 65

1. Heat a grill plate to hot.
2. Season the strips well with salt and pepper.
3. Cook them a minute or less each side – they should at least be pink. Test them by carefully cutting into one to judge if it needs a few more seconds. Serve with the sauce.

Guinea Fowl with Pancetta and Fennel

Based on a recipe from the River Café Easy Book, this is a useful all-in-one dish that can be prepared and refrigerated – ready to cook later in the day. Some brown basmati rice goes well with this.

2 large fennel bulbs – outer layers removed and sliced vertically into thinnish pieces
1 large red onion – prepared as the fennel
4 cloves of garlic – finely chopped
6 slices of pancetta – chopped
2 tbsp rosemary needles – chopped
4 tbsp olive oil
salt and pepper
1 guinea fowl – cut into 8 pieces (you can use ready prepared pieces), surplus fat removed
1 large glass white wine
8 more slices of pancetta

1. Heat the oven at 200°C/400°F/Gas Mark 6.
2. In a large bowl, combine the fennel, red onion, garlic, chopped pancetta, rosemary, olive oil, salt and pepper.
3. Turn over the guinea fowl pieces in the mix to coat them thoroughly. Transfer them to a roasting pan large enough to hold them in a single layer. Pour over a little more olive oil. Roast this in the oven for 30 minutes.
4. Add the white wine, and lay the remaining pancetta slices over the contents. Continue roasting for a further 15–20 minutes.

Ismail's Spicy Chicken Curry

Serves 4-5

Ismail Merchant was the producer half of the Merchant Ivory film-making team; James Ivory directed the films. I was in their film *The Europeans*, which was filmed in New England. He was truly a magician and a lifeforce; and a great cook.

Serve with brown basmati rice and perhaps broccoli.

3 tbsp olive oil
1 large onion – chopped
6 peppercorns
1 medium cinnamon stick
4 cardamom pods
6 cloves
2 bay leaves
1 chicken – cut up into 8–10 pieces and skinned
¼ tsp turmeric
½ tsp chilli powder
½ tsp ground coriander
½ tsp ground cumin
½ tsp ground ginger
2 cloves of garlic – crushed
salt to taste
125 ml/4 fl oz yogurt
½ tsp ground allspice

1. Heat the oil in a medium casserole.
2. Add the onion, peppercorns, cinnamon, cardamom pods, cloves and bay leaves. Cook until the onion browns up a little. Remove it to a plate.
3. Put the chicken pieces in and brown them, turning them often. Return the onion to the casserole.
4. Add the turmeric, chilli, coriander, cumin, ginger, garlic and salt to taste. Cook for 5 minutes, stirring occasionally.
5. Add 425 ml/15 fl oz hot water. Cover the pan and simmer until the chicken is just cooked – about 20 minutes.
6. Stir in the yogurt and allspice, and cook for another 5 minutes.

Quail Roasted in Balsamic Vinegar

Serves 4

Based on one of Anna del Conte's recipes which I must have used 50 times! It's simple and good for small company. We are lucky to have wonderful fat quail farmed near here. Serve over chickpea purée.

8 quail – heads off and washed and dried
salt and pepper
olive oil
100 ml/3½ fl oz/½ cup stock
3 tbsp balsamic vinegar
30 g/1 oz butter

1. Heat the oven at 200°C/400°F/Gas Mark 6.
2. Season the quail thoroughly with salt and pepper.
3. Heat some oil in an ovenproof pan and brown the quail on all sides.
4. Dribble 2-3 tablespoons of stock over the birds and put them in the oven. They will take between 15-25 minutes to cook, depending on their size. Baste them a couple of times and halfway through dribble a couple of tablespoons of the balsamic vinegar over them.
5. Test their doneness by gently pulling a leg away from the body: it should come away easily and the flesh be turning from pink to light brown.
6. Park the quail in a warm dish and deglaze the pan with the remaining balsamic over a gentle heat. Add a couple more tablespoons of stock to the pan and reduce the liquid a little. Add the butter in small pieces and stir in well. Pour some of this over the quail and the rest into a serving jug.

Delicious Roast Chicken

Serves 4

Every cook has a version of this classic. This one is based on Jamie Oliver's simple, tasty and robust recipe.

Serve with the Green Sauce on page 59.

1 free-range chicken
olive oil
salt and pepper
6 bay leaves
3 cloves of garlic – unpeeled and whole
1 lemon – halved
1 glass white wine

1. Heat the oven at 190°C/375°F/Gas Mark 5.
2. Rub the olive oil all over the chicken and season well. Stuff the cavity with the bay leaves, garlic and lemon halves.
3. Roast the chicken for 1½ hours. Halfway through take it out of the oven and baste it. When it is cooked, it should be nicely browned and the juices should be clear, not pink.
4. Take the pan out of the oven. Pick up the bird with a pair of oven gloves and up-end it, letting the juices run back into the pan. This is a little tricky but worth it for the taste of the gravy. Tip the pan carefully and spoon out excess fat/oil, leaving a spoonful in the pan. Add the glass of white wine and scrape any residue sticking to the pan. Gently stir over a lowish heat for 2–3 minutes. You can add some stock or more wine to make it go a little further. Taste and pour into a warmed jug.

9
Meat

Meat – in this case, beef, pork and lamb – does not play a leading role in our day-to-day eating scenario. We eat it and enjoy it occasionally. How times have changed. "Meat and two veg" I remember being the mantra of what we aspired to eat every day in the 1950s, as my father aspired to earning £1,000 a year – wow!

Red meat was good for a growing boy. I suppose this emphasis on getting enough meat to grow up "healthy, wealthy and wise" was a reaction to the long years of rationing when people ate no meat or very little for years.

Now we must limit our intake of red meat, it's said, and make sure we eat our five portions of vegetables and fruit a day. Sounds good to me. But a slice or two of pork fillet with a spoonful of its balsamic onion sauce (page 140), or a helping of the slow-cooked leg of lamb (page 146) with Mint Sauce with Apple and Onion (page 60) sounds good too – from time to time.

Grilled Lamb Chops

The timing for cooking does depend on the thickness of the chops of course.

4 lamb chops
4 tbsp olive oil
bay leaves/rosemary/thyme – any one or all
a couple of cloves of garlic – finely sliced
2 lemons
salt and pepper

1. Leave the chops to bathe in the oil, herbs, garlic and the juice of one of the lemons for a couple of hours.
2. Heat a grill to hot.
3. Place the chops on it and leave for 3 minutes without moving. Turn over and salt and pepper the uncooked side. Cook for a further 3 minutes. For a pinkish finish, the chop should spring back after you press it gently with your index finger.
4. Quarter the second lemon and offer the pieces for squeezing over the succulent chops.

Pork Chops and White Beans Baked in Orange Juice

Serves 4

This lovely autumn/winter comfort dish is based on one by the talented Frances Bissell.

2 x 400 g/16 oz tins/bottles white beans
4 spare rib chops (*échine* in France – these are the tastier ones)
1 onion – sliced
1 stick celery – sliced
2 oranges
1 tsp coriander seeds
150 ml/5 fl oz/½ cup stock
salt and pepper
chopped fresh coriander or parsley

1. Heat the oven at 160°C/325°F/Gas Mark 3. Put the beans in the oven dish you will serve from.
2. Brown the chops well in a non-stick pan. Lay on top of the beans.
3. Brown the onion and celery in the same pan – the fat from the chops will be enough to fry them in. Lay them on the chops.
4. Carefully cut some strips of zest from one of the oranges. Bury these in with the chops and beans. Squeeze the juice from the oranges over the chops.
5. Crush the coriander seeds and sprinkle over. Add the stock.
6. Cook in the oven for 2 hours. Check after an hour that there is enough liquid, but be careful not to add too much or the concentrated taste of the sauce will weaken. Season when cooked. Sprinkle over the coriander/parsley.

Lamb Tagine

This superb dish for company is adapted from one in Frances Bissell's exceptional book *The Pleasures of Cookery.*

2 kg/4½ lb boned shoulder of lamb – cut away as much fat as possible, ending up with about 1.5 kg/3½ lb lean lamb, cut into 2 cm/1 inch cubes

3 tbsp olive oil

3 onions – sliced

4 cloves of garlic – chopped

1½ tsp cumin seeds

1½ tsp coriander seeds

850 ml/1½ pints/3½ cups stock

24 dried apricots – halved

salt and pepper

parsley, or even better coriander – chopped

2 large tins flageolet beans – drained and rinsed

1. Heat the oven at 160°C/325°F/Gas Mark 3.
2. Seal the meat in hot oil, using a large frying pan. When nicely browned, remove it to the ovenproof casserole you will serve it from.

3. Gently fry the onions and garlic in the fat and oil left in the pan, without browning them.
4. Fold in the whole spices and let them cook a little.
5. Add almost all the stock, leaving just enough in which to heat up the beans, and let it reduce a bit.
6. Add the apricots. Season this mixture and pour it into the casserole. Add a handful of parsley or coriander.
7. Heat the beans in a little stock and when hot add to the casserole. Turn everything over carefully. Bring it all to a simmer and place it low down in the oven. Cook for 2 hours, checking after an hour to see if it needs topping up with stock – being careful not to lose the intensity of the sauce.
8. Serve over bulgar wheat.

Pork Loin Roasted in Balsamic Vinegar

Serves 4

This is a very versatile dish adapted from one in the first River Café cookbook. It is good for company – you could cook two 1.5 kg/3 lb pieces of loin side by side; it would take no longer and you would have enough for twelve at least.

It goes very well with the White Bean Gratin (page 173) which you can cook in the oven while the pork is resting, covered in foil, for half an hour.

1 kg/2¼ lb pork fillet – rind and most of the fat removed
salt and pepper
50 g/2 oz butter
2 tbsp olive oil
2–3 good size red onions – cut into thickish slices, top to bottom
1 good tbsp rosemary – chopped
350 ml/12 fl oz balsamic vinegar
60 ml/2 fl oz red wine

1. Heat the oven at 220°C/425°F/Gas Mark 7.
2. Season the meat well. Brown it thoroughly on all sides, on a cast-iron grill if possible. Set it aside.
3. Put a roasting pan on medium to low heat.

4. Add the butter and oil, and gently soften the sliced onions for 5 minutes (not too long or they'll burn up too easily when in the oven).

5. Stir in the rosemary. Add the pork and half the balsamic vinegar. Turn the pork in it until it is well coated.

6. Put the pan in the oven and roast the pork for between 35 and 40 minutes – depending on the thickness of the fillet, it's best to check it at 35 minutes as you want to keep it moist but not too pink. After the first 10 minutes, turn the pork and onions briefly in the sauce. Five minutes before taking the pork out, add the remaining balsamic vinegar. The onion may look rather burnt – adding the balsamic moistens it again, in principle anyway!

7. Then out with the pork and let it rest, covered with foil. Deglaze with the wine and balance the taste – you may need a bit more wine.

8. To serve, slice the pork really thin and add some sauce to each plate with extra in a sauceboat on the table. I usually put three pieces on each plate.

Pot Roast Pork with Dried Mushroom and Juniper Berries

Serves 4

Marcella Hazan says that the best part of the pig for this delicious autumnal recipe is the hand or *jarret* in France. You can use fillet as well, but try to get hand; it is tasty and cheap.

I serve it over a mash of white beans, using the same method as for chickpeas on page 169.

30 g/1 oz dried mushrooms – cepes or porcini, cheaper ones will do too
1 small onion – finely chopped
6 tbsp olive oil
1 kg/2¼ lb boned hand of pork – trimmed of fat, and cut into bite-size pieces
8 tbsp white wine
2 tbsp wine vinegar
4 anchovy fillets – finely chopped
2 bay leaves – torn
25 juniper berries – crushed
salt and pepper

1. Soak the mushrooms in 400 ml/14 fl oz/1½ cups warm water for 30 minutes.
2. Lift the mushrooms out of the water carefully, chop and set aside. Filter the water into a bowl through kitchen paper and reserve.

3. Sauté the onion gently in 4 tbsp of oil, in a pot large enough to hold all the pork, until it colours a little. Now put in the pork and brown on all sides over medium-high heat.
4. Add the wine and vinegar and let them bubble for a couple of minutes.
5. Put in the mushrooms, their liquid, the anchovies, bay leaves and juniper berries, with a couple of good pinches of salt and plenty of ground pepper. Stir carefully and cover tightly.
6. Simmer very gently over a very low heat for 1½–2 hours. Check after an hour that there is enough liquid.

Sausages in a Red Pepper, Caper and Rosé Sauce

Serves 4

This is a recipe from a town not far from us, and with pink as a theme I discover! It uses Toulouse (known as *la ville rose* on account of the local brick) sausage (pink before cooking), our local renowned pink garlic – *l'ail rose de Lautrec* – and the vin rosé of Gaillac. It's adapted from a recipe in Jeanne Strang's delightful book on the food of south-west France, *Goose Fat and Garlic*.

1 large red pepper
1 kg/2¼ lb good sausages – seek out your favourite and best, pricked ready for cooking
2 medium onions – chopped
6 large cloves of garlic – chopped
1 large tsp chickpea flour
1 flat tbsp tomato purée
2 glasses vin rosé
1 tbsp capers – squeezed
salt and pepper

1. Cook the pepper in boiling water for 10 minutes.
2   Remove and when cool enough slice it open, deseed it and cut it into medium dice.
3. Brown the sausages gently in their own fat over medium-low heat for about 20 minutes. Set aside.
4. Soften and lightly colour the onions and garlic in the same pan.
5. Sprinkle over the flour and mix it in with the tomato purée. Pour in the wine, stirring the while. Add the capers, and the pepper, stir these for a few moments, before adding the sausages. Season with salt and pepper, and continue cooking for 10 minutes.
6. Serve over simple quinoa – not pink.

Slow-Cooked Shoulder of Lamb

Serves 4-5

Based on a wonderful recipe by Skye Gyngell. Serve with the courgettes (on page 73) mixed into the meat.

1 shoulder of lamb
sea salt and black pepper
2 fresh bay leaves
1 bunch sage
1 dried red chilli – crumbled
2 anchovies
5 cloves of garlic
2 large glasses white wine
2 tbsp red wine vinegar

1. Heat the oven at 170°C/325°F/Gas Mark 3.
2. Carefully trim the shoulder of most of its fat. Season it well with salt and pepper.
3. Brown it in a large pan over medium-high heat. It's not easy to do this as the shoulder is a difficult shape that doesn't lend itself very easily to this – do the best you can.

4. Transfer it to a large baking tray. Add the bay leaves, sage, chilli, anchovies and the whole garlic cloves. Pour over the white wine and vinegar. Cover the tray with foil – it's important to do this carefully – otherwise you may find that the liquid dries up over the long cooking time. Place on the middle shelf of the oven.

5. Cook for 2^1/$_2$ hours. You might check it after 1^1/$_2$ hours to see if the liquid needs adding to.

6. Remove the foil and cook for a further 30 minutes to brown the meat a bit more. Ten minutes before the lamb is ready, cook the courgettes, as per page 73.

7. Remove the lamb from the oven (it should be soft enough to eat with a spoon). Pull the meat from the bone, discarding the shoulder blade, and arrange on a serving platter. Add the courgettes. Sprinkle over some parsley and serve.

Slow Roast Leg of Lamb

Serves 6-8

The White Bean Gratin (page 173) and Mint Sauce with Apple and Onion (page 60) go well with this recipe, adapted from the River Café Cookbook, as would some roast tomatoes.

3 kg/6½ lb leg of lamb
garlic slivers to lard the leg
olive oil
salt and pepper
200–250 ml/½ pint/1 cup milk

1. Heat the oven at 210°C/410°F/Gas Mark 6.
2. Make slits in the fat side of the lamb. Insert the garlic slivers – I don't think you can have too many, the tedium of doing it sets in after a while though! Rub the lamb all over with olive oil and salt and pepper.
3. Put the lamb in its roasting tray into the oven and roast it for 15 minutes. Then lower the heat to 150°C/300°F/Gas Mark 2 and cook for 3 hours.
4. Take the lamb out and place onto a warm plate and cover it with foil. Skim the fat off the juices. Place the pan over medium heat on top of the stove. When it is very hot, add the milk. Stir and scrape all the good bits stuck to the pan. Lower the heat and cook it gently until the resulting sauce is a lovely nutty brown.

Sausages Cooked with Red Cabbage

Serves 4

Another handy winter dish originating from Marcella Hazan. It's all in one; you don't need anything else expect plenty of the mustard of your choice, although you could follow it with a crisp green salad.

10 tbsp olive oil
2 cloves of garlic – chopped
1 kg/2¼ lb red cabbage – quartered, stemmed and finely sliced
1 kg/2¼ lb good pork sausages
salt and pepper

1. Put the olive oil and garlic in a large sauté pan or casserole (something that will hold the initially bulky pile of cabbage) and fry gently until nicely golden.
2. Add the cabbage and turn it well in the oil and garlic. Let it reduce gently, turning it from time to time while the cabbage cooks.
3. Put the sausages in a frying pan. Brown them all over.
4. When the cabbage has reduced (this can take about 30 minutes of gentle cooking), add salt and pepper and the sausages. Cook them together, the sausages buried in the cabbage, for another 20 minutes, turning them over from time to time.

10
Pasta

Sunday night has developed into pasta night chez nous; it's a sort of night off for me – not from cooking, rather from planning, and pasta is a wonderful standby.

All it takes is a packet of spaghetti, spaghettini or penne, a tin of tomatoes and a clove of garlic.

We eat wholewheat pasta – which is on the shelves of most supermarkets these days – and prefer it. It's still a rarity in restaurants – though I was brought out of a jetlag daze recently when I spotted one at the end of the pasta offerings on a menu in New York City.

How al dente it's cooked is a matter of taste. In Italy you'd think it was an arrestable offence to overcook pasta – they cook it al very dente and it makes for agreeably slower eating.

I tend to get stuck with "the ones we love!" but here are a few more of the endless possibilities...

Broccoli Pasta

This is a great pasta – a little different and it takes a bit of organizing of ingredients beforehand – but well worth it.

salt
1 kg/2¼ lb broccoli – cut into small florets
450 g/1 lb short dry wholewheat pasta, such as farfalle or
    penne
5 tbsp olive oil
2 cloves of garlic – thinly sliced
8 anchovy fillets – mashed up
3 small chilli peppers – finely chopped with their seeds
50 g/2 oz freshly grated Parmesan cheese
1 tbsp dry roasted pine nuts
50 g/2 oz toasted breadcrumbs – wholewheat or rye

1. Bring a large saucepan full of water to the boil – salt well.
    Cook the broccoli in the water until it's just tender. Lift it out
    and into a warm bowl.

2. Bring the broccoli-scented water back to the boil, slip in the pasta and stir it once to stop it sticking to the bottom.

3. Heat the oil in a small pan and add the garlic. Cook it on a low heat to avoid it burning. When it begins to colour, take the pan off the heat and add the anchovies, stirring to make a sauce – add a tablespoon of the hot water to help it meld.

4. Add the chillies and put the pan back on a very low heat.

5. When the pasta is ready, drain it and return to the hot saucepan. Add the broccoli and the sauce to it. Turn everything over, carefully coating the broccoli and the pasta in the oily sauce.

6. Heat the serving bowl and fold the mixture into it.

7. Sprinkle the cheese, the pine nuts and the breadcrumbs on top – to be mixed in after you have presented the dish triumphantly to the company!

Pasta "Puttanesca"

Serves 4

Pasta "hot woman" is what we've always called it – *puttana* being Italian for prostitute. One story has it that these women of Naples would leave a pot of pasta in the window to tempt the men inside; another that it's quick enough for them to make and eat between clients. I think it's too good to rush! It's up to you how hot you make it. This version is adapted from Claudia Roden's recipe in her *The Food of Italy*.

3 cloves of garlic – chopped
5 tbsp olive oil
chopped chilli pepper – perhaps 2–3 small ones
450 g/1 lb tin tomatoes – drained of half their juice
   or 450 g/1 lb fresh tomatoes
50 g/2 oz capers – squeezed
100 g/4 oz anchovy fillets – very finely chopped
100 g/4 oz juicy fat Greek olives – pitted
bunch of parsley – chopped
400 g/14 oz pasta – wholewheat spaghetti, spaghettini, linguine

1. Fry the garlic in 2 tablespoons of olive oil until it colours.
2. Add the chilli and then the tomatoes, the rest of the oil, and the capers, and cook gently for about 30 minutes.
3. Carefully fold in the crushed anchovies, and let them meld into the sauce for 5 minutes.
4. Add the olives and the parsley and cook on for about 5 minutes.
5. Cook the pasta in plenty of well salted boiling water to your taste. Drain and put in a heated serving bowl. Pour over the sauce and mix thoroughly.

Penne with Rosemary and Balsamic Vinegar

Serves 4

This is another one adapted from *Marcella's Kitchen* and is a year-round wonder. It is quick and simple to do and has a distinctive earthy flavour, thanks to the rosemary. It's worth taking care to slice the garlic very thinly.

4 cloves of garlic – very thinly sliced
8 tbsp olive oil
2 sprigs rosemary or 2½ tsp dried rosemary
600 g/20 oz tinned tomatoes, i.e. a large tin – drained of juice
salt and pepper
400 g/14 oz penne or farfalle or mix of the two
2 tsp balsamic vinegar

1. Sauté the garlic gently in the oil with the rosemary (if using fresh) until the garlic sizzles.
2. Add the tomatoes, salt and plenty of pepper. If using dried rosemary, add it with the tomatoes. Cook for 10–15 minutes.
3. Cook the pasta in well salted water.
4. Drain the pasta and add to the sauce. Cook a minute or two – turning the pasta in the sauce. Turn off the heat and make a well in the middle of the pasta and add the balsamic vinegar. Again turn the pasta thoroughly in the sauce.
5. Serve with fresh grated Parmesan cheese.

Spaghettini with Cinnamon and Bay Tomato Sauce

Serves 4

Unexpected ingredients for a pasta dish but it works. You can use tinned or fresh tomatoes – but fresh and ripe are better. Anna del Conte says it comes from Umbria.

1 large onion – chopped
4 tbsp olive oil
450 g/1 lb tomatoes – chopped with some of their juice
¼ tsp cinnamon
10 fresh bay leaves
salt and pepper
400 g/14 oz wholewheat spaghettini

1. Using a large frying pan, sauté the onion in the oil until it softens – don't brown it.
2. Add the tomatoes, the cinnamon and the bay leaves. Season well and cook gently for about 20 minutes.
3. Cook the pasta in a large saucepan of salted water. Test for doneness and drain, retaining a little of the water.
4. Transfer the pasta to the frying pan, adding a couple of tablespoons of the water. Turn it over and mix well and cook for a minute or two. This is usually served without cheese – but that's up to you.

Spaghettini with Pesto Sauce

Serves 4

This epitomizes summer suppers. Of course, you have to make the pesto sauce (page 61) beforehand but that might be in the fridge already; resting with a film of olive oil on top to preserve it. The only tricky thing is keeping everything warm. Heating the plates helps.

I like to eat this on a warm summer night outside — with extra olive oil and Parmesan.

400 g/14 oz wholewheat spaghettini
1 tbsp olive oil
decent amount of pesto sauce — 4 tablespoons perhaps
a tablespoon of the pasta water to loosen the sauce
Parmesan cheese to grate
olive oil available to pour over if you fancy

1. Cook the pasta in plenty of salted boiling water.
2. When it's done – and before draining it – spoon some of the water into a bowl.
3. Put the cooked pasta into a heated serving bowl, add the tablespoon of oil and turn the pasta in it.
4. Loosen the sauce with a little of the reserved water, and add it to the pasta, turning it carefully to coat it.
5. Serve immediately with Parmesan cheese. You could sprinkle some parsley on top.

Spaghettini with Tuna and Tomato Sauce

Serves 2

Based on Anna del Conte's simple and delicious recipe, in which the tinned tuna is uncooked. It's good to use lovely ripe tomatoes in summer; but tinned tomatoes are better the rest of the year. These quantities might stretch to 4 as a starter, in which case add another 100 g/4 oz of pasta.

1-2 cloves of garlic (I like 2) – sliced
6 tbsp olive oil
450 g/1 lb ripe tomatoes – peeled and chopped
   or 1 x 400 g/14 oz tin of tomatoes – drained and chopped
10 black Greek olives – stoned and cut in strips
1 tbsp capers – drained and squeezed
salt and pepper
a dozen fresh basil leaves
   or a good tablespoon of chopped parsley
200 g/7 oz spaghettini
200 g/7 oz good tinned tuna – drained

1. Put the garlic in a small pan with half the olive oil, the tomatoes, the olives and the capers.
2. Bring to the boil and add some salt and the basil or parsley. Cook at a gentle simmer for 10 minutes or so. While this is happening, boil a large pan of water, salt it and add the pasta.
3. Drain the tuna into a serving bowl, and add the remaining oil and plenty of pepper.
4. When the pasta is done, drain it, reserving a little of the liquid to loosen the sauce if necessary and add it to the tuna.
5. Pour over the tomato sauce and mix it all well.

Tuna Pasta

Serves 4

This is rather a winter month's tuna pasta and very comforting. Most of the ingredients are cupboard-based staples.

6 tbsp olive oil
2 cloves of garlic – chopped
3 tbsp parsley – chopped
400 g/14 oz tin of tomatoes – chopped
400 g/14 oz wholewheat spaghettini
salt and pepper
400 g/14 oz tinned tuna (drained weight) – broken up
50 g/2 oz butter

1. Heat the oil in a small pan and add the garlic.
2. When it begins to colour, add the parsley and stir for 30 seconds. Add the chopped-up tomatoes.
3. Cook for about 25 minutes, until the sauce gains an unctuous quality.
4. Bring a large pan of water to the boil and salt it. Add the pasta and cook it until it's done to your taste. Some like it more al dente than others; you have to keep testing it.
5. While the pasta is cooking, add the tuna to the sauce and mix it in thoroughly. When it's hot, add the butter and let it melt in. Season well – lots of pepper.
6. Drain the done pasta and put it in a warmed bowl and add the sauce. Mix the two thoroughly and serve on warmed plates.

Spaghettini with Walnut, Garlic and Parmesan Sauce

Serves 4

Frances Bissell's take on this lovely pasta dish. The taste is more authentic if you shell the walnuts yourself, but you need a little time. You could give the task to a guest who says, as guests sometimes do: "Is there anything I can do?"!

100 g/4 oz shelled walnuts – be careful, if you shell them yourself, to avoid any teeth-cracking bits being left in
2 cloves of garlic – crushed
1 tbsp parsley – chopped
salt and pepper
5 tbsp olive oil
1 tbsp walnut oil
100 g/4 oz freshly grated Parmesan cheese
400 g/14 oz wholewheat spaghettini
a little extra parsley

1. Put the first three ingredients in a food processor, season with salt and pepper, whizz to a smoothish sauce by adding the two oils gradually. Check the seasoning. Remove to a bowl then fold in the Parmesan.
2. Cook the pasta in plenty of boiling salted water. Drain it, keeping a little of the liquid, and put it in a thoroughly heated bowl. As with the pesto pasta (page 157), it is a challenge to keep the pasta hot. Loosen the sauce with some of that liquid – a tablespoon or two – being careful not to flood it and lose the flavour.
3. Pour the sauce over the pasta and turn it over and over. Sprinkle some chopped parsley on top.
4. Serve in warm bowls with more olive oil and Parmesan to hand.

11

Grains and Pulses

I like lentils; the same goes for white beans and chickpeas – all pulses in fact – brown basmati rice and quinoa too. But I can understand that for some they are a poor substitute for potatoes. In fact, they can offer rather more than the simple spud. I recently read this on the website Passion for Pulses under the title "Pulses and Diabetes":

"Pulses have a low glycemic index, making them excellent sources of carbohydrate in the diet of those affected by diabetes... Once referred to as 'poor man's meat' because they are high in protein and inexpensive, pulses are valuable additions to a modern diet [way of eating] because of their good taste, convenience, ease of use and nutritional role in managing and preventing diabetes."

They have many uses and take on board countless flavourings. Some pulses, such as lentils and beans, have a reputation for making you flatulent. Well, it's true, no denying, but for me their tastiness outweighs this minor inconvenience; but that's an individual choice. Meredith, for instance, takes some persuading.

Comfort Lentils (otherwise known as Dal)

Our friend, Tari Mandair (we call him the Carefree Cook, and he is an example to all us worryguts) is never panicked when people turn up unexpectedly and have to be fed. He looks to see how many extra guests are coming through the door and adds more water to the dal accordingly.

We often eat these lentils with broccoli simply steamed and brown basmati rice.

If there is some left over, form it into little burger shapes, coat them with some chickpea flour and fry in hot oil.

500 g/1 lb red lentils
1 litre/1¾ pints/4 cups vegetable stock (I use a vegetable stock cube per 500 ml)
4 tbsp vegetable oil
1 medium onion – chopped
1 tsp coriander seeds – pounded in a mortar and pestle
1½ tsp cumin seeds – pounded in a mortar and pestle
1 tsp garam masala
½ tsp chilli powder

1. Rinse the lentils very thoroughly – until the water shows clear.
2. Put them in a saucepan with the stock and bring gently to the boil. Turn the heat down to low and let them simmer, covered, stirring from time to time. They are done when a small puddle floats on the top. Turn them off.
3. Heat the oil in a small frying pan. Add the onion and fry until it is browning nicely.
4. Add the spices and mix them in well. Cook on gently to release the aroma.
5. Add the cooked spices and onion to the lentils and mix in thoroughly. Heat through and serve.

Gratin of Fried Chickpeas with Chorizo and Spinach

Serves 4

Adapted from a recipe by Mark Bitman of the *New York Times*, this is a great one-pan dish. This version should be enough for a light lunch for 4, though the first time I made it Meredith and I polished off the whole lot! It could also serve as a delicious starter served over salad.

4 tbsp olive oil
450 g/1 lb bottled or tinned chickpeas – rinsed, drained and dried thoroughly
salt and pepper
100 g/4 oz spicy chorizo sausage – sliced and diced
250 g/8 oz spinach – washed and shaken dry
60 ml/2 fl oz/4 tbsp sherry
2–3 handfuls of wholewheat/rye breadcrumbs
extra olive oil

1. Heat 3 tablespoons of olive oil in a pan large enough to hold the chickpeas in one layer.
2. When hot, put in the chickpeas, season and turn down the heat a little. The object is slowly to crisp them up – allow about 10 minutes for this – shaking the pan from time to time and being careful not to let them burn.
3. When they have coloured nicely, add the chorizo and cook on in the same way for about 8 minutes. Empty the mix into a bowl.
4. Return the pan to the heat, add the remaining tablespoon of olive oil, the spinach, some seasoning and the sherry sprinkled over. Turn the spinach over and over as it melts, and, once the liquid has evaporated, return the chickpea/chorizo mix to the pan and fold in the spinach.
5. Transfer this mix to a small gratin dish, sprinkle over the breadcrumbs and the extra olive oil. Put under a hot grill for about 3 minutes. Serve with a salad.

Flageolet or White Beans with Tomato, Sage and Garlic

Serves 4

The little green flageolets go well with a lamb chop or two and the white version with sausages or a pork chop.

1 clove of garlic – chopped
2 tbsp olive oil
½ tsp dried sage or a sprig of fresh sage
2 tinned tomatoes squashed in a little of their juice
½ vegetable stock cube dissolved in 3 tbsp hot water
1 tin/bottle flageolet beans – drained and rinsed
salt and pepper

1. Lightly colour the garlic in the olive oil over a gentle heat.
2. Add the sage and stir a couple of times.
3. Add the tomatoes and let them cook gently for about 7 minutes.
4. Add the halved stock cube and the beans, and stir them in well, then cover and cook very gently for 10 minutes to let everything meld nicely. Add a little more hot water if things start to dry out.
5. Season with salt and plenty of pepper.

Chickpea Mash

Serves 4

This is delicious and a really useful accompanying vegetable.

2 bottles/tins chickpeas
1 clove of garlic – crushed
½ tsp chilli powder
salt and pepper
4 tbsp olive oil

1. Put the chickpeas, garlic, chilli powder, salt and pepper in a food mixer.
2. Add the oil and whizz.
3. Add more oil if it's still too stiff.
4. Put the mix in a saucepan and gently heat it to hot. It will loosen up as it heats through.
5. Adjust the seasoning.

Brown Basmati Rice

Serves 2

Basmati rice has a "medium" glycemic index (between 56 and 69), making it more suitable for diabetics. Organic rice is the best to use.

½ coffee mug organic brown basmati rice
1 mug (same size as above) cold water
bay leaf
1 tsp salt

1. Put the rice in a small saucepan with the cold water. Bring slowly to the boil.
2. When the water starts to roll, put in the bay leaf and the salt, cover and turn to very low. It will take about 30 minutes – you should be able to smell when it is nearly done; Meredith says that you should never take the lid off. Check for doneness.

Puy Lentils with Labneh and Dry Roasted Walnuts

Serves 6

You can serve this tepid as a salad or warmer as part of a meal, with salmon fillets, leaving out the labneh and walnuts. Goat's cheese is a good alternative to labneh.

250 g/8 oz puy lentils – washed thoroughly
Enough water to cover the lentils by an inch (2.5 cm)
1 small onion – peeled and cut in half
2 cloves of garlic – peeled
Sprig of thyme and 2 bay leaves
1 tbsp red wine vinegar
4 tbsp olive oil
salt and pepper
1 large spring onion – chopped small (optional)
50 g/2 oz shelled walnuts – dry roasted
2 tbsp labneh or goat's cheese

1. Put the lentils in a pan with the water, onion, garlic, thyme and bay leaves. Bring it to the boil and simmer, covered, until the lentils are just done; about 25 minutes, depending on the age of the lentils. If you leave them too long, they will be mushy – you may have to top up with more water.
2. Drain the lentils – ditching the herbs, the onion and garlic – and place them in a serving bowl.
3. Add the vinegar and the olive oil and turn them in carefully. Season with salt and pepper to taste.
4. Sprinkle the spring onion (if using), walnuts and labneh or goat's cheese (a couple of tablespoons, say) on top.

Quinoa with Sautéed Vegetables

Serves 4

This very useful and delicious alternative to rice comes originally from the Andes. You can cook it plain in stock or as here a little more interestingly. To re-heat cold quinoa, steam for a couple of minutes.

225 g/8 oz quinoa
570 ml/1 pint/2½ cups vegetable stock
1 medium red or yellow onion – chopped
1 clove of garlic – chopped
1 small red pepper – deseeded and cut into small dice
1 small chilli – deseeded and cut into small dice
1 small courgette – cut into small dice
1 medium tomato – peeled, deseeded and cut into small dice
4 tbsp olive oil
salt and pepper

1. Cook the quinoa gently in the vegetable stock, covered, until you can fluff it up with a big fork – about 15–20 minutes.
2. Meanwhile, put the vegetables in a pan and sauté them gently in the oil until soft.
3. Add the vegetable mix to the cooked quinoa. Season to taste with salt and pepper but be careful with the salt as the stock will have some salt in it. It's good to let the flavours meld a little. Mix in carefully and eat hot or cold.

White Bean Gratin

This is a good accompaniment to Slow Roast Leg of Lamb (page 148) or the Pork Loin (page 140). It would serve vegetarians with a vegetable at the same meal.

1 kg/2¼ lb prepared (i.e. either from dry or tinned or,
    preferably in my view, bottled) white beans
3 generous tbsp crème fraîche
salt and pepper
2 generous tbsp grated Parmesan
2 generous tbsp dry wholewheat breadcrumbs
25 g/1 oz butter

1. Heat the oven at 200°C/400°F/Gas Mark 6.
2. Put the drained and rinsed beans in a bowl.
3. Add the crème, salt and pepper to taste. Don't stint on the former, you need enough cream to avoid them drying out in the oven but not so much that they are overwhelmed. Mix carefully and thoroughly. Check the seasoning – a delicious exercise! – the pepper especially.
4. Arrange the beans evenly in a baking dish (preferably one that presents well at the table).
5. Mix the Parmesan and breadcrumbs well – adding some salt and pepper.
6. Melt the butter. Pour it over the breadcrumbs and Parmesan, and mix thoroughly. Cover the beans with the mix.
7. When you are ready, put the gratin in the oven for about 20-30 minutes. It should be nicely browned on top and sizzling.

Farinata or Socca (Pancake)

Serves 4

This is street food and is still sold on the streets of Nice and Marseille in southern France. These pancakes are about 20 cm/8 inches wide and are good for parking things on – a fried egg or some bacon bits or, as I did recently for a light supper, thinly sliced roast tomatoes.*

170 g/6 oz chickpea flour
400 ml/14 fl oz/1½ cups sparkling water
80 ml/2.5 fl oz/⅓ cup olive oil
salt and pepper
1 tbsp rosemary leaves
olive oil

1. Put the flour in a mixing bowl. Add the water and whisk it in until smooth.
2. Add the oil and whisk it in. Add pinches of salt and pepper and the rosemary. You will have roughly half a litre (20 fl oz) of batter. Leave to soak for 20–30 minutes.

3. When you are ready to make the pancake, heat a swirl of olive oil in a 25 cm/10 inch frying pan. When hot, put a tablespoonful of the stirred mixture in the pan and turn the heat down a little. Cook for a few seconds until you can ease the pancake loose with a spatula or fish slice. Now you have to turn it over! Be bold! Practice makes perfect and anyway the first attempt, if not completely successful, will be edible. Cook the pancake a further few seconds and remove from the pan. Both sides should be a golden brown. Add a few twists of the pepper mill on each.

For a larger pancake, carefully pour a second tablespoon of batter on top of the first.

* Cook, sprinkled with a little salt and olive oil, for 20 minutes in a low oven (140°C/275°F/Gas Mark 1).

12
Tips

A Less Tearful Way of Chopping Onions

First couple of times, keep the sticking plaster at hand!

1. Peel the onion.
2. Halve it top to toe.
3. Lay one half flat with the root-end facing away from you. Starting at the right side and with the tip of a sharp knife, cut down just above the root. Then work your way over the dome to the left side with similar cuts. Hold the half firmly with your left hand, swivel it, keeping it in shape and with the knife in your right hand carefully cut into the onion low and horizontally. Do the same several times as you climb over the dome.
4. Lastly you cut down the vertical – working from right to left and, voila, you have a chopped onion!

Home Roasted Nuts

Healthier, tastier and cheaper than the bought variety and also quick and easy to do. They are a conversation starter too.

250 g/8 oz raw cashews
1 tsp olive oil
sprinkling of fine salt

1. Heat the oven at 180°C/350°F/Gas Mark 4.
2. Put the nuts in a bowl. Add the oil and turn and turn until all the nuts are coated. Sprinkle in some salt and turn again. Cover a shallow baking tray with foil. Lay out the nuts in a single layer.
3. Roast for 10 minutes, in the middle of the oven, and check for doneness: eat one gingerly. They should be a light golden – like the commercial ones! Cook a little longer if you need to.
4. Leave them to cool off and try not to eat them all at one sitting.

250 g/8 oz raw almonds

• Follow the same method as above but they may need an extra 10 minutes' cooking. Do check them though – burnt nuts aren't nice!

Simple Herb Teas

- We have a mad mint patch – which starts to show some time in late March and lasts through October. It is unstoppable and a great source for a great sauce (page 60).

  For an infusion of tea, all you need is a couple of leaves in a cup or pot with boiling water poured over.

  Leave it to infuse for a minute or so and you have a wonderfully fresh-tasting drink. You can do the same with thyme, rosemary and sage; root ginger too – so much nicer than a teabag!

Tip for Frying Sausages

- Fry for about 20 minutes, and for the last 10 splash a tablespoon or two of white wine in the pan and add some chopped herbs (rosemary, thyme, sage, parsley, oregano).

How to make Labneh (Yogurt Cheese)

Makes a fair amount

1 x 1 litre/about 30 fl oz or 8 x 125 ml/4 fl oz pots of 0% fat yogurt
a cut square of muslin
a sieve
string

1. Spread the muslin over a sieve and press it down. Place the sieve over a medium bowl.
2. Carefully de-pot the yogurt into the muslin.
3. Gather the square together, so the yogurt forms a ball. Twist the muslin round in order to tie it. You can help the process along with a gentle squeeze or just leave the yogurt ball to drip for a couple of hours into the bowl, preferably in the fridge. It will reduce surprisingly in volume – how much depends on how thick you want it. Try it a few times.
4. You could put the yogurt straight into the sieve and over a bowl into the fridge but this will take longer – 12 hours perhaps – as you obviously can't squeeze the liquid out.
5. Then you can paint on this canvas by adding garlic, olive oil, black olives, herbs, etc. If it has become too dry, just mix in another pot of no-fat yogurt.

Index